④ £2.50

W43

you and your mid-adolescent

other titles in the You and Your Child Series
Editor, Dr A. H. Brafman

you and your baby: a baby's emotional life
Frances Thomson Salo

you and your toddler
Jenny Stoker

you and your child: making sense of learning disabilities
Sheila and Martin Hollins

you and your mid-adolescent

the hour of the stranger

James Rose

You and Your Child Series
Editor, Dr A. H. Brafman

KARNAC

First published in 2007 by
Karnac Books Ltd.
118 Finchley Road,
London NW3 5HT

British Library Cataloguing in Publication Data

A C.I.P. for this book is available from the British Library

ISBN-13: 978-1-85575-451-5
ISBN-10: 1-85575-451-7

10 9 8 7 6 5 4 3 2 1

Edited, designed, and produced by Communication Crafts

Printed in Great Britain

www.karnacbooks.com

contents

acknowledgements

Illustration on p. 57: From cover of *The Boys' Crusade* by Paul Fussell (London: Weidenfeld & Nicolson, 2004). Reprinted by permission of the publisher, Weidenfeld & Nicolson, an imprint of The Orion Publishing Group.

Figure 5.1 and Tables 5.1, 6.1–6.4: From J. Coleman & J. Schofield, *Key Data on Adolescence* (Brighton: Trust for the Study of Adolescence, 2003). Reprinted by permission of Jane Scholfield.

Figure 5.2: From S. G. Millstein, A. C. Petersen, & E. O. Nightingale (Eds.), *Promoting the Health of Adolescents* (New York: Oxford University Press, 1996). Reprinted by permission of Oxford University Press.

Extract on pp. 58–59: From D. W. Winnicott, "The Antisocial Tendency". In: *Through Paediatrics to Psychoanalysis*. London: Hogarth, 1958. By permission of Paterson Marsh Ltd on behalf of The Winnicott Trust.

Lyric on pp. 91–92: *Jet Song*. Words by Stephen Sondheim. Music by Leonard Bernstein. © Copyright 1956, 1957, 1958, & 1959 The Estate of Leonard Bernstein & Stephen Sondheim. Universal Music Publishing Limited. All Rights Reserved. International Copyright Secured. Reprinted by permission.

about the author

James Rose is a psychoanalyst. Since 1987 he has worked as a psychoanalytic psychotherapist at the Brandon Centre for Counselling and Psychotherapy for Young People, which is situated in Kentish Town, London. The author hereby acknowledges all those adolescents and young adults who gave him the experience upon which this book is based.

series editor's foreword

DR A. H. BRAFMAN

It is perhaps easy to classify the years from 14 to 17 as representing a person's mid-adolescence, but these are extremely complex years in a youngster's life and certainly very difficult years for the parents. Describing the problems faced by both adolescent and parents is, however, quite a daunting challenge for anyone. James Rose has drawn on his rich experience of working with adolescents and their parents to compose a sensitive, detailed, and most helpful analysis of the struggles that characterize these middle years of the process of adolescence. We live today in times of social instability and change, but James has managed to put the mid-adolescence we know in these times of uncertainty within a historical perspective that introduces a sense of hope that must be very helpful to the readers of this volume.

There is a central philosophy uniting all the volumes in the You and Your Child Series. Each of the authors featured has published papers and books for the academic and clinical communities; the present volumes, however, are specifically aimed at parents. The intent is not to convince but to inform the reader. Rather than offering solutions, we are describing, explaining, and discussing the problems that parents meet while bringing up their children, from infancy through to adulthood.

We envisage that two groups of parents may choose to read these books: some may wish to find here answers to specific questions or to problems they are facing in their lives, whereas others may read them only to broaden their knowledge of human development. Our intention is that the writing should be phrased in a way that might satisfy both groups. There is an attempt at something of a translation of what children of different ages experience in their lives with parents, family, and the wider world. Our authors have based their texts on their extensive work with children, adolescents, and their parents—not only in the authors' private consulting-rooms, but also in schools, community agencies, and teaching hospitals—and, in most cases, with children of their own.

The authors aim to depict the child's experiential view of his life, helping parents to understand behaviours, thoughts, and feelings that the child may not have been able to verbalize. There is no question of being the child's advocate—no purpose is seen in trying to find who is to blame for the problems under discussion. These are, rather, interested and knowledgeable professionals attempting to get child and parents to understand each other's point of view. In our books, the authors describe in detail the increasing range of each child's developing abilities on the path from infancy to adulthood: it is this knowledge of potential and actual abilities that is fundamental for an understanding of a child's behaviour.

Many, if not most, of the books available on child development adopt the view that a child is the product of the environment in which he is brought up. To some extent, this is obviously true: the child will speak his parents' language and adopt the customs that characterize the culture in which the family live. The commonly heard remark that a particular child "takes after" a parent or other close relation bears out the fact that each growing individual responds and adapts to the milieu in which he lives—and not only in childhood, but throughout his life. Nevertheless, it is still true that not all children brought up in one particular home will show the same characteristics. From a scientific point of view, there are endless discussions on the issue of nature versus nurture. However, from a pragmatic point of view, it is certainly more correct and more useful to consider family problems with children as being the result of an interaction—who started this, and when and how it started, is virtually impossible to establish. Through their words and behaviour, child and parents continually confirm each other's expectations; they keep a vicious circle going, where each of them feels totally justified in their views of themselves and of each other.

It is not rare that the parents present quite different readings of what each of them considers their child's problems to be. Needless to say, the same can be found when considering any single issue in the life of an ordinary family. The baby cries: the mother thinks he is hungry, whereas the father may feel that here is an early warning of a child who will wish to control his parents' lives. The toddler refuses some particular food: the mother resents this early sign of rebellion, whereas the father will claim that the child is actually showing that he can discriminate between pleasant and undesirable flavours. The 5-year-old demands a further hour of television watching: the mother agrees that he should share a programme she happens to enjoy, whereas the father explodes at the pointlessness of trying to instil a sense of discipline in the house. By the time the child has reached puberty or adolescence, these clashes are a matter of daily routine. . . . From a practical point of view, it is important to recognize that there is no question of ascertaining which parent is right or which one is wrong: within their personal frames of reference, they are both right. The problem with such disagreements is that, whatever happens, the child will always be agreeing with one of them and opposing the other.

There is no doubt that each parent forms an individual interpretation of the child's behaviour in line with his or her own upbringing and personality, view of him/herself in the world, and past and present experiences, some of them conscious and most of them unconscious. But—what about the child in question? It is not part of ordinary family life that a child should be asked for *his* explanation of the behaviour that has led to the situation where the parents disagree on its interpretation. Unfortunately, if he is asked, it can happen that he fails to find the words to explain himself, or occasionally he is driven to say what he believes the parent wants to hear, or at other times his words sound too illogical to be believed. The myth has somehow grown that in such circumstances only a professional will have the capacity to fathom out the child's "real" motives and intentions.

It is an obvious fact that each family will have its own style of approaching its child. It is simply unavoidable that each individual child will have his development influenced—not *determined* but *affected*—by the responses his behaviour brings out in his parents. It is, however, quite difficult for parents to appreciate the precise developmental abilities achieved by their child. No child can operate, cope with life, or respond to stimuli beyond his particular abilities at any particular point in time. And this is *the* point addressed in the present series of books. We try to provide portraits of the various stages in the child's cognitive, intellectual, and emotional development and how these unfolding stages affect not only the child's experience of himself, but also how he perceives and relates to the world in which he lives. Our hope is that establishing this context will help the parents who read these books to see their child from a different perspective.

you and your mid-adolescent

1

introduction

What is adolescence?

Mid-adolescence is hard to define in terms that are objective and unambiguous. The onset of early adolescence is much easier both to conceive of and to recall because it is clearly associated in most people's minds with the arrival of puberty. Puberty can begin at any time between the ages of 9 and 14 years. If you cast your mind back to your own teens, you might recall moments when it seemed that you or the world would never be quite the same again. Such a realization may have been associated with an ill-defined thrill or a dread—or, maybe, both at the same time. These feelings may have centred about senses of the physiological changes and growth of your body, or your feelings about a girl or a boy of a similar age, or a sense of change in how you were recognized and regarded by others important to you.

But other changes also set in which influence a young person because not only do they acquire a body with new powers and sensations, they also begin to think about the world and the people in it in a new way. This will affect how they feel about themselves and others. D. H. Lawrence described adolescence as the "Hour of the Stranger", emphasizing perhaps not only the strangeness of the new sexually potent body but the sense that an early adolescent experiences attractions to others that have a new meaning, coupled with the sense that life will never be the same again.

With memories like these in mind, we can go straight into thinking about the main psychodynamic changes that occur in adolescence and its main developmental tasks.

Paul van Heeswyck (1997) summarized these tasks as follows.

- moving away from the close and familiar security of home and school to the wider variety of people and ideas in the world at large
- ownership of the body, which was previously held under a kind of leasing arrangement with the parents—this involves integrating into the body image the newly awakened sexual feelings and fantasies, as well as rapid changes in size and strength
- the attainment of personal autonomy and becoming a separate person—this is usually taken to mean the establishment of a confidence in and a responsibility for one's beliefs and actions
- the achievement of intimacy with others, based on secure personal boundaries and a fixed sexual identity
- adaptation to the adult world of work and care of the young, with the twin values of the identification and pursuit of personal and career goals and commitment to agreements entered into and tasks undertaken

D. H. Lawrence anticipated this list as follows:

> The child before puberty is quite another thing from the child after puberty. Strange indeed is this new birth, this rising from the sea of childhood into a new being. It is a resurrection which we fear.
>
> And now, a new world, a new heaven and a new earth. Now new relationships are formed, the old ones must

> retire from their prominence. Now mother and father inevitably give way before masters and mistresses, brothers and sisters yield to friends. This is the period of *Schwärmerei*, of young adoration and of real initial friendships. A child before puberty has playmates. After puberty he has friends and enemies.
>
> A whole new field of passionate relationships. And the old bonds relaxing, the old love retreating. The father and mother bonds now relax, though they never break. The family love wanes, though it never dies.
>
> It is the hour of the stranger. Let the stranger now enter the soul.
>
> And it is the first hour of true individuality, the first hour of genuine, responsible solitariness. A child knows the abyss of forlornness. But an adolescent alone knows the strange pain of growing into his own isolation of individuality. [Lawrence, 1923]

In many ways these tasks have been set in motion during early adolescence and will certainly not be completed during the mid-adolescent years specified above. It might therefore be worth asking what the point is of identifying a mid-adolescent phase. There will only be a point if something identifiable and unique happens in these years. Some say that this is the time when parents experience the most difficulty in being parents to their growing children. This struggle of being parents is, in some ways, reminiscent of the "terrible twos" of toddlerhood. In many ways the issues are very similar—a growing sense of self and the discovery of the word "no", the growing awareness and control of the body, and the dawning sense of the other as other, coupled with growing language attainment.

We therefore have to ask whether—when we talk about adolescence—we are talking about a biological maturational process or a social construct brought about by socio-economic conditions. According to Reed Larson (2002): "Adolescence, as it is generally known, is a Western invention of the late nineteenth and early twentieth century. The societal context for its invention was urbanization, the development of secondary education and the desire to remove youth from the labour market." Another, simpler way of putting it is to suggest that our society has had to create a stage during which the individual is no longer a child but is, alas, not yet an adult. We create an elaborate rite of passage to take account of the complexities of modern life and call it—adolescence.

What can we say about mid-adolescence?

It might be said that adolescence as a process is the result of a conflict of expectations between developing individuals and the society in which they live. Its onset can be defined by arrival of puberty, but its termination is much more difficult to define objectively. For this reason, it often makes more sense to talk about a process of *adolescing*, thus coining a new verb to describe a process that begins at puberty but perhaps never quite finishes until death. All those around the adolescent will be affected, be they the family, friends, or representatives of authority. Thus, although the adolescent can feel alone in a quite new way, their new reactions to this experience will impinge upon all around.

At a societal level, this has given rise in the last century to the notion of a "youth culture"—as if this process of adolescing were a new social development and young people today pioneers of a new order. This was perhaps the consequence of starting to realize that different cultures manage the process of transition from childhood to adulthood quite differently. While the idea of adolescents being pioneers might be gratifying to some adolescents, we can be pretty sure that the experience that something new happens when puberty "turns up" is not a new phenomenon that first occurred in the twentieth century.

One of our earliest known written inscriptions shows that concern about adolescence has been with us for a long time. King Hattusili of the Hittites wrote, in about 1620 BC, as a father to his son of 13:

> Keep thy father's word and stay away from wine in favour of bread and water while in youth, but when old age is with thee drink to satiety. And then thou may'st set aside thy father's word.

One may pause to ponder on all the hard work that went into preserving these thoughts for posterity. It was clearly important, but it quite possibly means that the son was a long way from observing his father's admonitions. Three thousand years later Shakespeare reflected comparable feeling when he, in the words of the shepherd in *A Winter's Tale,* described this period thus:

> I would there were no age between ten and three-and-twenty, or that youth would sleep out the rest; for there is nothing in the between but getting wenches with child, wronging the ancientry, stealing, fighting. [Act III, Scene 3]

If modern parents recognize some of their own feelings in these words, it suggests that adolescence is not quite such a recent invention as some might imagine. Certainly, we get a sense of young people of this age doing things that are disapproved of by their parents and by "ancientry" in general. However, although these behaviours may sometimes seem as meaningless today as they seemed to the ancientry of the past, this book is intended to explore what these activities might mean to young people themselves, in the hope that the anxieties of those responsible for these young people can be addressed.

Perhaps Winnicott (1968) captured the dilemma for adolescents and their parents in the following words:

> What I am writing here (dogmatically in order to be brief) is that the adolescent is immature. Immaturity is an essential element of health at adolescence. There is only one cure for immaturity and that is the passage of time and the growth into maturity that time may bring.
>
> Immaturity is a precious part of the adolescent scene. In this is contained the most exciting features of creative thought, new and fresh feeling, ideas for new living. Society needs to be shaken by the aspirations of those who are not responsible. If the adults abdicate, the adolescent becomes prematurely, and by false process, adult. Advice to society could be: for the sake of adolescents, and of their immaturity, do not allow them to step up and attain a false maturity by handing over to them a responsibility that is not yet theirs, even though they may fight for it.

These very widely quoted words are often misunderstood—as if they meant that adolescence and immaturity are to be equated. The implication might be that, given time, adolescents will grow out of or through any difficulties that they might have—all that is necessary is the passage of time, and not a lot else. But looking at the full text reveals that this is far from what Winnicott said. He warns that there will inevitably be a struggle between adults and adolescents about issues to do with responsibility and authority. Adults, as parents, will fail their adolescent children if they hand over a responsibility for which the latter are not yet ready. Hence, the adolescent's struggle for this responsibility will, in turn, create a conflictual and ongoing turmoil for the parents. This is the difficulty of being a parent to an adolescent: parents will inevitably be confronted with the reality of their own adolescence—with all its successes and failures—providing a model for how they exercise their own authority in the role of being parents. At no time is this truer than in the mid-adolescent years, because the adolescent's struggle to actualize their own authority now gets going at a time when the immaturity of childhood is still very apparent.

How does mid-adolescence impact upon us as adults?

This struggle occurs in very familiar arenas: for example, when the adolescent goes out with friends at night, there is the perennial question of the time when they are expected to be home. There is the matter of the balance between leisure interests and schoolwork. There is the question of allowances, pocket money, and the time needed to do a job, which brings a little additional money at the expense of time for other important matters, like homework. There is the matter of boys' and girls' growing sexuality and, for the parents of teenage girls, the question of when their daughters need contraceptive services. For the parents of teenage boys, there is the matter of helping them with the reality of the risks of unprotected sexual activity. Then, there will be questions in parents' minds about the company their adolescent children keep, particularly once they "discover their social life". All sorts of anxieties about what they are getting up to—and with whom—will emerge and be the source of angry exchanges as the parents react to the increasing difficulty in controlling both their own anxieties and their children. Parents can need a great deal of help during these years. Sometimes this can simply be the opportunity to compare their own experience with that of others in the same situation. Sometimes, however, professional help is needed.

How this book is organized and why

For these reasons, this short book has been organized in the following way. We begin with looking at the emotional and intellectual development that is usually observed during these years. By "usually", I am referring to a sense of what is normal. We need to keep in mind, however, that around that "norm" there is usually a considerable range of variation. But given this variation, there is a sequence of development through which all must go in one way or another. Above all, this development supports the capacity to begin and maintain relationships.

We follow this by looking at the tremendous variation that can be observed in physiological development following the arrival of puberty and what this can mean for the developing adolescent. We then turn to how important the peer group is for the mid-adolescent and the reason why this seems to provide so many of the signifiers of adolescence.

Having looked at the broad scope of development during mid-adolescence, we can then think about the difficult—and sometimes distasteful—experiences that mid-adolescents, and their parents, may have to face. As a background we have to consider the current framework of the law as it concerns adolescents. In short, parents have to consider how to cope with the situations when things seem to go wrong. Some quite serious forms of disturbed mental behaviour and feeling emerge for the first time in adolescence and are desperately worrying for all concerned. From the beginning of adolescence onward, eating disorders, self-harming, and suicide occur increasingly often, reflecting the turmoil that some adolescents and their immediate families must endure.

As an essential counterpoise to this, it must be borne in mind that for many adolescence is a time of great happiness and fulfilment as parents witness their children reaching towards adulthood and enjoying their achievements in the process. But a book that seeks to be a help to those going through the process of mid-adolescence—from the point of view either of the adolescent or of families—must attend to the serious strains that may have to be borne if the picture portrayed is to have any realism. "Youth culture" may idealize the adolescent and vilify parents; but, as we shall see, the paradoxical expectations placed on both adolescents and their parents arise from the creative tension between the desire to progress and the desire to regress as mid-adolescents consolidate the move out of childhood and prepare for adulthood—no easy task for mid-adolescents, nor for those responsible for them!

2

emotional and intellectual development: Romeo and Juliet

Considerable intellectual and emotional development occurs during the mid-adolescent years. John Santrock (1999) recalled an adolescent once saying, in a thoughtful way:

> "I began thinking about why I was thinking what I was. Then I began thinking about why I was thinking about why I was thinking about what I was."

This reflection on the process of thinking is an example of the new powers of thought that adolescents begin to develop. Quite why this happens is not known precisely, but we can link its emergence to other new developments during the early teen years. At first sight it would seem that this adolescent is now capable of being within himself and standing outside himself at the same time, with the result that his subjective experience is not totally dominated by what he can see from his own point of view: the potential is there to be able to see the world from others' points of view as well. In itself, this is not a new achievement at this age. This ability can easily collapse under the pressure of powerful feelings—particularly powerful feelings towards others, which can seem to the individual and those around them to be like a kind of paranoia. What is important in understanding mid-adolescents is being aware of the upsurge of powerful feelings towards others and how far they can maintain an ability to think about themselves instead of impulsively launching into action. When they cannot, the likelihood is that others will feel the effects.

A growing sense of the privacy of the self

We might also notice that observation in the extract above is of our adolescent's *sequence* of thought, which means that he can situate himself in time. We might link this with the impact of puberty, which, as the body changes its shape and function, accompanied by new feelings and experiences of others, forces a sense of *"what I once was"* and *"what I will become"* on the consciousness of the mid-adolescent. Time, therefore, registers itself in new way, giving a sense of a past and a future and thus an experience of memory (or history) and desire—(the future).

After this, we might notice Santrock's adolescent's use of the word "I", which implies a new kind of subjective experience, or a capacity for one—indicating reflection upon the self. This is experience considered and, as the adolescent reflects on his experience, he becomes the object of his own thought. The capacity to think of how another person might think has probably already been developed. It has been observed that young children develop a "theory of mind" when it comes to thinking about other people—that is, young children will start to think about *how* others think, not just *what* they think. But when these powers are applied to the self, a new depth of thought and experience is possible, giving rise to a different sense of self.

It is important to remember at this point that the onset and pattern of this development is unique to each individual. This makes any attempt to tie the emergence of these developments to chronological age of dubious value. At worst, it can have the connotation that earlier, or sooner, is better—with the result, for example, that those whose puberty "turns up" later than that of their peers can feel at some disadvantage and in some way inferior and in some sense ashamed.

A growing sense of the body . . .

The changes in the shape of the body brought by puberty and noticeable in the self and in others lend new significance to the importance of appearance and image. The mirror can, therefore, constantly be resorted to as a source of anxiety—or, on the other hand, of reassurance. With the idea of an image or "me, as others see me" comes the emergence of an ideal self, or a "me, as I would like to be". We might wonder whether the passion for designer labels at this stage suggests an effort to bury differences in appearance and size under a uniform of "cool".

We can see now that an important consequence of the adolescent's capacity to reflect upon his own thought is the new way in which he can see himself in time and in a social world of other people—of either sex. However, because of the extent of individual difference seen at this age, we should beware of assuming that such a development will be universally observed in all adolescents. Furthermore, some adolescents are much more communicative than others. We may not know much about what goes on in the adolescent mind simply because they do not tell us. They may consciously choose not to disclose it, or they may find it awkward to tell us about their experience precisely because their capacity to reflect on their experience is so new to them.

. . . and of others

With the new experience of self can come a much greater sensitivity to being intruded upon by others. No better marker is there of the emerging essential privacy of the adolescent self than their bedroom. How it is used can provide a clue to this experience but, more particularly, to its emotional impact upon the parents. It would be a mistake to draw too many conclusions from what is directly observable, because we must remember that, as adults, what we perceive in our adolescent children will reflect our own hopes and fears for them as much as anything that might be "objective". Such is the nature of perception, particularly when we are as emotionally involved with what we see as we can be with our adolescent children.

The kind of cognitive development we are thinking about here was first described by Jean Piaget, a Swiss psychologist, as the emergence of *formal operational thought* (Piaget, 1950). As this develops, so thinking becomes capable of being abstract instead of being rooted in the concrete realities of everyday life. As an example, we might think of the difference between arithmetic and algebra: the same operation can be performed in different situations about different things. It can also be more logical and be capable of thinking of hypotheses—or of what might be—and the means of confirming—or otherwise—these hypotheses. Hence the capacity to think about *what might be* opens the door to thinking of ideals. In consequence, adolescents can be idealistic in a new way and may, consequently, be disappointed when they realize how they, and those around them, fall short of their expectations. They may also become angry and resentful when they see how the world seems to fall short of their ideals.

Piaget's ideas have been challenged by the extent of individual variation in the capacity for formal logical thinking. There seems little doubt that this capacity is heavily determined by culture and education. Consequently, helpful as these thoughts are, there seems to be a sense that they describe what mid-adolescents might be able to do rather than what they might experience. We can see how Piaget's ideas help *us* to imagine an adolescent's experience. But it might help us further if we could see how the use of the kind of logical thinking described by Piaget might affect *the adolescent's experience of dealing with others*. However, rather than describe the form of thinking in the sense of naming it, it might help us to grasp their experience and to think about it in different way if we stop and think about how different forms of thinking determine what kind of experience we can have.

To do this, let's think about "a prisoner's dilemma", which takes the form of a game of logic.

A prisoner's dilemma

Here I am using the prisoner's dilemma as a way of thinking about adolescents' experience as they go through the adolescing process and the part played by peers in the process of becoming an adult. We have to try to account for some of the psychological tasks faced by every individual as they develop from the onset of puberty to adulthood. This will help us to think about the difficulties encountered as they negotiate these tasks and why these difficulties take the form that they do. To aid our reflection on the subjective dilemmas of adolescence, I propose we use this problem to see what we might learn from how it can be solved.

The game is this:

A prison warder has selected three prisoners, and he tells them that one of them is to be released. In order to choose the one to be released, they will have to submit to a test. The warder has five disks, three white and two black (which he shows the three prisoners).

He tells them that he will fasten one of these disks to the back of each prisoner, so that it is out of his own field of vision but not that of the other two. The test is that the first to pass through a door and state the correct colour of his disk will be released. This must be done by logic and not by probabilistic guesswork. The warder then fastens one of the three white disks to the backs of each of the three prisoners. The black disks are not used at all.

The solution to the problem works from the numbers of black and white disks.

There are only three possible combinations of the black and white disks—black, black, white (b b w); black, white, white (b w w); and three whites (w w w). It is therefore possible for each prisoner to look at the backs of the others and realize that if he sees two black disks then his must be white. The first possibility is therefore excluded, because each person sees two white disks.

In the *first logical moment, or instant, of looking*, all that can happen is the exclusion of certain possibilities. We look, but we cannot yet understand.

In the *secondary time of understanding*, each prisoner can think (having first excluded b b w as a possibility): "If I were black, the other two whites I see would waste no time realizing they are whites." Hence, in this phase, each must think of what the others are thinking. For a prisoner to distinguish the logical possibilities, the answer *lies in the hesitation of the other two subjects*. We can see that the adolescent thinking about his thinking cited above can also use his skills in thinking about what others are thinking—or, for that matter, not thinking.

In the *third, logical time of conclusion*, each prisoner can think: "I hasten to declare myself white, so that these whites whom I consider in this way do not precede me in recognizing themselves for what they are." Hence the moment to conclude represents an assertive judgement that the subject makes about himself, in which he emerges from identification with the other into the individuality of subjecthood. It is the prisoner who realizes that the others do not yet know what they are—because they do not act—who thereby knows and declares himself to be white.

What on earth has this got to do with understanding adolescents? Let us now look at the solution to the dilemma. From the logical solution to this problem, we might formulate three stages, which do, of course, have a temporal sequence, but there is no necessary sense of *chronological* time implied by this sequence. You may have had a sort of "ah-ha" moment as you worked out the solution to the problem. This experience of discovery can be used to understand something of how adolescents *discover who they are.*

These stages can be given titles and be linked to what can be observed as adolescents develop physiologically and psychologically:

1. *The moment of the look:* the onset of puberty. We know that at puberty there is certainly a subjective sense of looking different and feeling different, and that the body does new things. In addition, others—of either sex—look different, as are one's feelings about them. But it seems that much has to be learned by each individual about what these differences mean, and this does not occur in an instant. Nevertheless, for many—if not most—there is a sense of a moment after which life is never the same again.
2. *The time for understanding:* establishing identifications and differences. Solving the problem relies on entering the minds of the others via a kind of trial identification. This is not done deliberately or necessarily consciously, but it becomes possible when, like the adolescent above, one can be within one's experience and observing it at the same time. The importance of the peer group and social contact beyond the family has long been established. It is also a matter of daily observation to note the importance

to mid-adolescents of wearing the "right gear", the absence of which seems to guarantee exclusion on the basis of not being seen as "cool". Almost anything that serves to demarcate the group—be it clothing or an activity—will do for the purpose: the point is that it is public and noticeable. This can be written off as simply a kind of empty, strutting display, but thinking about the peer group as permitting the experience of identification and the exploration of difference at the same time gives it a very serious significance.

3. *The moment to conclude:* In the logical game, the subtlety lies in the fact that the similarity of the prisoners is discerned on the basis of their hesitation—or what they do not do—rather than what they actually do. Not until the similarity is grasped can the problem be solved from observation of the others' inertia. The capacity to say "who I am" is the result of the development of an ability to identify and discern difference. This capacity for identification is not the same as identification with the peer group, where the identity of the individual is submerged as a means of obscuring the reality of differences. We are talking here about a trial identification, which permits us to see the position of the other without being dominated by it. It is clear that this is a more sophisticated form of identification, rather akin to empathy.

If we use these ideas to think about the developmental process of adolescence, we might see its relevance more clearly if we think about the development of sexual behaviour and feelings towards others. Later on in this book there is a chapter entitled "having sex, having intercourse, and making love". This title comes from an observation by doctors working in a centre for adolescents offering birth-control and family-planning advice. They found that young adolescents (12–14 years) would often talk about their sexual experience in terms of "having sex". Mid-adolescents would talk about "having intercourse", whereas late adolescents would talk about "making love".

This everyday observation, which cannot be said to be systematically objective in the scientific sense, is possibly a distillation of the doctors' experience of helping these young people. One doctor told me of the bleak feeling associated with the recall of the first sexual experience by an early adolescent. It seemed to be an activity of the body, devoid of the experience of something that happened with someone else or associated with any feelings of love. In this, of course, the doctor was describing her own feelings, aroused in reaction to hearing the early adolescent's account of the experience. The mid-adolescent talking about "having intercourse" moves the experience on from being simply an encounter of two bodies to one in which two people are involved, but who do not necessarily know one another, perhaps because they do not necessarily know themselves. Consequently, the partners identify with one another through being engaged in an activity called intercourse, and in that moment there is no difference between them. They are using each others' bodies for the pursuit of their own pleasure, but there is no exchange between them. This only comes when adolescents talk about "making love" and the idea of giving and receiving something new enters the conception of the situation—that is, that two separate people are involved, and each complements the other. This requires a great deal of emotional development.

Adolescent passion: the case of Romeo and Juliet

Romeo and Juliet is a play about two young people we might think about as mid-adolescents in fifteenth-century Verona. Juliet is clearly identified as being 14 years old. The abiding appeal of the play suggests that it explores themes to do with growing up that touch people of different cultures in different eras, suggesting something more universal, rather than something culturally rooted in Renaissance Italy. I refer the reader to Katherine Dalsimer's (1986) brilliant exploration of the use of literature in exploring female adolescence. Leonard Bernstein's successful transposition of the theme into *West Side Story* is surely confirmation of this contention.

Above all, *Romeo and Juliet* is a play about adolescent passion. It is also a play in sympathy with the plight of the lovers who, by falling in love with the enemy of their respective families, enact the psychological conflict at the heart of adolescent love. One's first love is inevitably the enemy of one's family, for it is through this experience of first love that the power of early family ties is loosened.

It is interesting to note that Shakespeare's source for the story was Arthur Brooke's 1567 poem, "The tragicall Historye of Romeus and Juliet". In his preface, Brooke says that he is setting out to show

> A couple of unfortunate lovers, thrilling themselves to unhonest desire, neglecting the authoritie and advice of parents and frendes . . . attemptyng all adventures of peryll for thattanyng of their wished lust . . . abusing the honourable name of lawefull marriage, the cloke the shame of stolne contractes, finallye, by all means of unhonest lyfe, hastyng to most unhappy death.

Decidedly, therefore, Brooke takes the position of Juliet's father, who sees his daughter as a possession who must do his bidding and marry the parentally chosen Paris. This gives us the chance to look beyond the predicament of the adolescent breaking away from family ties and to see the predicament in which parents find themselves. For, in order to enable the adolescent to feel that separation from the family is indeed necessary in order to achieve maturity, the parents' resistance must be, in some sense, intentional and real. There is no room for play-acting here.

Shakespeare invites us to think of the experience of the passion of adolescent love and to see some of its determinants. We see two warring families—Capulets and Montagues—and the process, in four short days, of Romeo Montague and Juliet Capulet meeting, falling in love, betrothing themselves to one another, and dying. The play delineates the choices that each of the main characters must make, and each choice has a connotation of death associated with it. Romeo and Juliet must cut their family ties if they are to be joined together. Thus, for each, the choice of partner is with the enemy of their family. To their parents, their choice of each other is unsuitable, and the place in the play of the desirable suitor—for Juliet Paris, and for Romeo the shadowy Rosaline—is to represent the pressure of parental ambition for the adolescent.

We can, if we so choose, write off the play as a portrayal of some curious antics peculiar to the upper middle classes in the historical and social conditions of Renaissance Italy. However, if we step back a bit and think of the choices that the characters give each other—and the consequences of the implied options—then I think we can see what a serious business we witness in the play, and why death is used so effectively as a dramatic tool.

In essence, each choice invites the choosers to give up being what they are and to become someone that they either might be expected to fear to be or do not want to be. This links with the prisoner's dilemma, where the solution to the problem lies in seeing the inertia of others, which represents their reluctance to see who they are. Seeing this difference solves the problem. For Romeo and Juliet, falling in love with each other forces them to confront their own differences from one another and from their families. But why does the play end in death? Is Shakespeare saying—in contrast to Brooke—that parents must let their children be different from them, or else the consequence is death? In this sense, death becomes a metaphor for a process that is awesomely irreversible. They must also accept their differences from each other for the same reason.

Sometimes these choices are put by the character to themselves in soliloquy. Thus, Juliet says:

> Romeo, Romeo, wherefore art thou Romeo?
> Deny thy father and refuse thy name.
> Or, if thou wilt not, be but sworn my love
> And I'll no longer be a Capulet. [Act II, Scene 2]

Later, she says:

> 'Tis but thy name that is my enemy;
> Thou art thyself, though not a Montague. [Act II, Scene 2]

With this, Juliet realizes that she and Romeo must renounce the ties to their parents that their names represent. There is a momentous choice before her. As if to underline this, Romeo's murder of Tybalt (a Capulet) makes this choice even more difficult and complicates Juliet's mourning of Tybalt because of her desire and fears for Romeo. Juliet's father is then portrayed as forcing the choice of Paris upon her, threatening expulsion from the family if she does not comply.

> Hang thee, young baggage, disobedient wretch!
> I tell thee—get thee to church a Thursday
> Or never after look me in the face. [Act III, Scene 5]

Thus, the thrust of the adolescent desire to break family ties has the result that they may come to see their parents as enemies and tyrants. This has nothing to do with the parents actually being tyrannical—it is simply the consequence of the young person striving to develop and possibly *unconsciously wanting to feel* the restraining force of the parents as they pull away from them—as they must and as society requires.

So, if we now go back to the prisoner's dilemma, we can see that the prisoner who notes his companions' inertia will only act on this if he wants to leave the cell. If Romeo and Juliet are to fall in love and marry, and thereby risk exclusion from home and hearth, then it must be because they want to be with each other and recognize that the consequence of their choice is the giving up of infantile ties with their parental figures.

Hence, there is a parallel with the prisoner in the dilemma. Romeo and Juliet must recognize in each other this complementary wish to leave childhood and the family. The poignancy of the lovers' death at the play's finish draws the audience back from the private worlds of the lovers and into the world of their parents, against which their love developed. On the surface there is no happy ending here . . . but only if we fail to remember that all the time the play seeks to portray to the "ancientry"—us . . . the audience—the reality of adolescent passion in all its progressive struggle against the regressive pull of childhood and the maintenance of infantile ties. Its subtlety is that it manages to do this from the points of view both of the lovers and of their parents. Thus, parents must give up their children, and children must give up their parents. This is both inevitable and irreversible. Death is an effective motif for this developmental change.

The impact of the cognitive changes observed earlier in this chapter makes possible the various emotional shifts that we have just discussed. In essence, we notice a progressive urge to adulthood and a regressive pull back to childhood.

We will now think about a number of arenas in which this paradox can be expressed and observed in the behaviour of mid-adolescents: in what might be called the "psychosocial disturbances" of adolescence. This will illustrate the feeling of young people at this age. But we cannot ignore the feelings of the older generations. The kind of socio-legal systems we have created for the reception of our adolescents into adult life will reflect both our desire to help them into the adult world but also, perhaps, our hatred of the fact that they will turn their backs on us—as Romeo and Juliet turn their backs on their families in their deaths—representing their entry into the adult world.

3

sexual development: having sex, having intercourse, and making love

We have already noted that, for the individual adolescent, puberty "turns up" at some time between the ages of 10 and 16. We might say that the arrival of puberty is the business of early adolescence, regardless of the chronological age at which it actually arrives. The business of mid-adolescence is the commencement of the process of absorbing the emotional consequences of the physiological changes that occur.

The impact of puberty

The change in the physiological body, entailing it now being sexually mature and capable of reproduction, is a momentous change in its psychological impact and its impact upon others. Because the body now looks different, people can easily expect the newly changed young person to be different. Different they will, of course, be—but not necessarily in the way that is expected. We can say that the task of early adolescence is to accept this new potency, and that of mid-adolescence is incorporate it into a new way of being with oneself and, in turn, being with others. This is partly because others will expect new things of the mid-adolescent. The title of this chapter is intended to summarize the tasks of sexual organization during adolescence, beginning with recognition that the young person is capable of having sex, but this is not seen as being something in which one engages with another person. One might say that it is thought of as an activity—at its most primitive—in which one engages with another person as a body, but the person of the other is not significant. The idea of intercourse introduces the idea of being with another person, and being sexual has a psychological significance as well as a physical one.

We are forced to consider adolescent experience in this way because of the enormous individual variation in both the onset of puberty and the time it may take for the individual to reach full maturity in a physiological sense. Hence each individual's experience is unique, and this makes it very easy to imagine that a young person's experience is common to our own. Societies other than our own have instituted *rites of passage* that make it easier for all concerned to be clearer about what can be expected of an individual before and after these thresholds. To a certain extent, the requirements imposed by the law are the nearest we get to these rites of passage, but they are by no means the same, not only because of the criminal consequences, but also because of the difficulty of enforcing them. Thus the age of so-called sexual maturity is 16 years, but the difficulty in convicting a 14-year-old boy of statutory rape of a girl of his own age is considerable, even in cases where pregnancy has resulted. And even when there is a conviction, what is a just punishment to be?

We can learn something about the subjective meaning of the onset of puberty from various statistical studies of the impact of puberty on boys and girls. In spite of the difficulties in obtaining accurate data, we do seem to be able to say that the chronological age of the onset of puberty has decreased significantly over the past century and a half. In Northern Europe and the United States, in the 1850s the average age of the onset of puberty was between 14 and 16 years; now it is around the age of 13. As with all averages, there is a significant range of variation, but there is still reason to believe that there has been a significant reduction in the statistical sense. There are many possible reasons for this reduction: standard of living, general health, quality of diet could all have something to do with it.

Next, we might consider what we know about gender differences in the way puberty seems to be welcomed. Despite considerable effort, technical difficulties have made the achievement of reliable results a problem. There has been a tendency to consider that boys regard the onset of puberty positively, whereas for girls the opposite seems to be true. This may be because studies have focused upon weight, which for boys means increased muscularity, pointing towards a more adult body, whereas girls experience an increase in weight to be less pleasing. To this might be added the undoubted monthly physical discomforts of the "curse".

What is perhaps of greater significance to the individual adolescent is that it seems that those maturing early seem more likely to get involved in activities typical of those who are older in the chronological sense—possibly before they are emotionally able to handle these. Studies carried out in the 1990s in Sweden suggested that so-called "early maturers" were led into "norm-violating activities". Thus, those maturing early were found to have been drunk about twice as frequently as were their later-maturing peers, when the age of the group under study was just over 14 years. By the time the group was nearly 16, this difference had disappeared. An instructive qualifier of these ideas has been that norm-violating activities were primarily related to the peer networks of early-maturing girls. These girls had older friends, who were seen as being more tolerant of norm-breaking behaviour than the friends of on-time or late maturers.

However, it is interesting that the potentially damaging effects of this apparent precocity seem to diminish rapidly once the individual enters late adolescence—a fact that seems to be true for both boys and girls. Despite this, it does seem that early-maturing girls are more at risk than those maturing later, mainly because of psychosocial conditions—that is, social conditions impacting upon a young person that have psychological significance to them. We have just mentioned the significance of the peer group and how this will affect young persons' sense of self and, to a certain extent, their values and aspirations.

Some facts about adolescent sexual behaviour

Of obvious relevance to the discussion here are the known statistical facts about sexual behaviour. In terms of conception rates in England and Wales, there seems to have been a small but steady increase from 1969 to 2000 in 13–15-year-olds. In 2000, 46% of pregnancies led to maternities and 54% to abortions. It is interesting to note that in the comparable period conception rates among 15–19-year-olds seem to have fallen marginally: in 2000, 39% of these conceptions led to abortions and the remainder to maternities.

That cultural factors partly determine these findings is indicated by a comparison of birth rates in 1998 in OECD countries for 15–17-year-old mothers: these showed the lowest rate for Japan (about 2 per 1,000), and the highest for the United States (just over 30 per 1,000). The United Kingdom (at over 16 per 1,000) led the European countries, with the countries with the lowest rates including Switzerland, the Netherlands, and Italy (at 3 or fewer per 1,000) (see Coleman & Schofield, 2003).

If we add to these figures what is known about sexual behaviour before the age of 16 from the "National Survey of Sexual Attitudes and Lifestyles", it seems that in the mid-1960s about 15% of boys and about 5% of girls owned up to first sexual intercourse by the age of 16. By 1998, these figures had increased to 30% and 25%, respectively (Wellings et al., 2001). Whether these differences are to be accounted for by a greater openness over the ensuing 35 years among this age group in general is not known. Equally, the extent to which the legalization of abortion, the liberalization of law concerning homosexuality, and much increased sexual health education have had an impact on these trends is difficult to establish objectively.

Putting all these figures together leads to an impression of the mid-adolescent of either gender currently being potentially increasingly sexually active and consequently being at risk of facing the adult responsibilities of child-bearing and -rearing before being psychologically ready—quite apart from before being economically ready—to do so. The enormous national differences noted suggest that cultural factors play a big part, even though it might be argued that these days differences are not so marked in today's mass culture as they would have been even five decades ago. In addition, there will be those who say: "So what? There is still the matter of personal responsibility. Whether someone gets pregnant or not is their own responsibility—not Society's."

Why a young woman becomes pregnant—happily or not—is often very difficult to understand, not least by the young woman herself. Treating it as a decision that is solely a matter of rational choice opens us to all our personal prejudices. It seems obvious that education, stable social conditions, and secure family structures bring traditions that pay full respect to relationships, child-rearing, and self-respect, enabling young people not to take on such awesome responsibilities before they feel ready. It also seems obvious that access to contraceptive services for young to mid-adolescents does no more than recognize, and respond to, the psychological and physiological reality of these young people.

In the midst of all this, of course, are the parents, who play a crucial part because they will inevitably and unavoidably act as role models for young people. They will play a crucial part in establishing the climate in which their teenage children prepare and equip themselves for their sexual lives. It is an involvement that cannot be avoided. Doing nothing is not an option: consciously or not, the young person concerned will make choices about how they will exercise their sexuality, and they will do so regardless of determined parental intervention, concern, or neglect. The belief that not talking about sexuality to your children means that you won't put ideas into their heads will not work in this case.

The dilemma of Gillick competence

A good practical example of this dilemma is the concept of "Gillick competence": it raises issues to do with parental responsibility, confidentiality, and what judgements those younger than 16 can be expected to make in their own interests. This brings in the question of whether a girl under 16 should be able to give consent, by herself, to medical treatment that may, in some cases, involve abortion. In 1986, Victoria Gillick brought these issues under the legal microscope when she did not want her daughters, who were under 16, to be offered contraceptive help without her knowledge. She won her case, and for the following year it was unlawful to provide contraception to young people under 16 who refused to tell their parents that they were requesting contraception.

The decision was subsequently reversed by Appeal in the House of Lords. The guidance the Law Lords gave established that "giving contraceptive advice to young people under 16 years does not necessarily infringe parental rights nor are the doctors, who act in good faith, committing the criminal offence of aiding and abetting sexual intercourse with young people under the age of 16."

Clearly what brought all this under the spotlight was the fact that Victoria Gillick did not want her daughters offered contraception without her knowledge. What became equally clear was that there are circumstances in which the young person concerned is unwilling to inform her parents or those acting *in loco parentis* that she is seeking contraception. According to the current guidelines, an obligation is placed on doctors or other professionals offering contraceptive advice and treatment to persuade a girl tell her parents, guardians, or those *in loco parentis* about the advice or treatment she is given.

But there is a recognition that there will be cases in which it is not possible to persuade a girl to so do. In these cases, doctors or professionals are justified in giving advice or treatment if they can satisfy themselves that:

1. the young person can understand the advice given and has sufficient maturity to understand what is involved morally, socially, and emotionally
2. the person will not inform her parents that contraceptive advice is being given and will not allow the doctor or professional to so do
3. that the young person will begin or continue sexual intercourse with or without treatment
4. that without contraceptive advice or treatment, the young person's physical or mental health would be likely to suffer
5. that the young person's best interests require the doctor or professional to give contraceptive advice and/or treatment without parental consent

These guidelines have come to be ironically known as the way for professionals to establish whether a girl can be considered to be "Gillick-competent". They have been drawn up to find a way through complicated situations that allow professionals to make the best medical assessments and treatments that they can *in the individual patient's best interests—both medically and psychologically*. By implication, to this might be added, "*. . . and not in anybody else's, even if they think it is their duty to disagree*".

This is a situation, then, in which "society"—in the shape of the law—has intervened very forcefully and expressed itself very clearly. If we transpose those very sensitive and difficult situations where there is a lack of parental consent to something young people feel impelled to do, then do we have another *Romeo and Juliet* situation, but this time not in fourteenth-century Verona but in the twenty-first-century modern world?

Nowadays the protagonists do not do battle with rapier, poison, and banishment: they are forced into potentially irreconcilable conflict through the consequences of the responsibilities brought by modern medical science. The technology has changed, but the feelings can remain the same and have the same consequences, because the issues are the same and have to do with the claim that all individuals make for their own decision making: that is, *their own minds* and the ownership of *their own bodies* to use as they will.

A case of an adolescent girl becoming pregnant

To explore these issues further, let us think about why a girl might become pregnant when contraception is readily available. Joanna Brien and Ida Fairbairn (1996) give an excellent summary of the various possible reasons for this. They note that in 1994 there were nearly 180,000 abortions, even though contraception has been widely available since the 1970s. They provide many reasons for resisting the temptation of being caught up in a moral panic—not least of these the fact that there is no form of contraception available is risk-free, and not just because the user is human and thus can be expected to err. They add that conscious awareness of the realities of fertility is often lacking. According to Ida Fairbairn, 25% of first appointments at the Brandon Centre in London, which offers birth control and family planning services to young people between the ages of 13 and 21, are for a pregnancy test. It has also been found that 80% of teenage mothers had not planned to get pregnant and had not used contraception (Guillebaud, 1993).

When we find that young teenage girls' and boys' presuppositions about their fertility are a curious mixture of wishful thinking and ignorance, we can only conclude that there is a desperate need for effective sex education. Young women still come to pregnancy advisory centres saying that they did not realize that they could get pregnant the first time they had sex, or when they were less than 16, or if they were drunk, or if they had sex standing up. A comparison of the UK experience with that of other countries is instructive. In Holland, for example, the age of consent is 12, rather than 16, as in the UK. Sex education is explicitly provided. Teenagers in Holland have one seventh of the UK conception rate, and the average age of first intercourse is marginally greater in Holland.

But these are figures and statistics that tell us something about teenagers as a group. They don't shed much light on the experience that can lead young teenagers to become pregnant. Brien and Fairbairn (1996) give the following example:

> Anna was just 16 when she came for a pregnancy test, which confirmed that she was indeed pregnant. She was tearful and the doctor was acutely aware of her deep concern for this young girl. She described an extremely unhappy home situation, comprising of her mother, little half-brother and mother's boyfriend of one year whom she hated. Anna's own father had disappeared when she was 2, she had made a good relationship with her step-father but he too had left three years ago. Anna got on OK with her mother until about ten months ago. Anna thought that this was when she started going out with James, whom her mother

disliked. Anna said that this was only because he was Black. Anna was hurt by this and was planning to leave home to get away from such racists. Anna's obvious love for James seemed to be an incredibly powerful statement of independence from the fetters of her childhood. However, focusing so intensely on her mother in the session, she also showed how entangled this relationship truly was.

This fragment of an experience provides a glimpse of the many possible factors that have a bearing on a young woman becoming pregnant. We note that the doctor feels deeply responsible for this young woman, suggesting that partly she seeks to be cared for by her parents, by whom she feels abandoned. We also see echoes of the *Romeo and Juliet* theme, with the Montagues and Capulets this time played out in racial terms. Of course, there is much we don't know, but we might guess that—for Anna—pregnancy represents a solution to an impossible home situation in that she feels profoundly at odds with the rest of her family. Getting pregnant, like leaving home, represents a way of getting away from the family and leaving behind an unhappy childhood. We do not know any more about Anna's mother than what Anna tells us: she may be as Anna describes her, she may not.

If we generalize these impressions to the experience of all adolescents and their parents, we can get very close to imagining the situation to be one in which young people—just like Romeo and Juliet—are struggling to break free from the shackles imposed on their freedom by their repressive parents. If we choose to identify in a simple way with the two of them, then we will see their parents as repressive.

What is not so easy to see is the possibility that this perception of the parents as not wishing their children to grow up could also be a reflection of the adolescent *reluctance to grow up*.

The truth is, of course, that the parties concerned rarely find themselves in situations of unequivocal certainty about their position. These situations come about partly because of the pressures of physiology and society, but the meaning of the situations in which individuals find themselves will be also partly influenced by their desire to retreat to the golden past—most obviously recognized or known as "*when I was a boy*" or, "*. . . a girl*".

The surprise is to find that this is sometimes experienced by parents and by mid-adolescents alike: they can all suffer nostalgic agonies, to their mutual amazement. Hence, an over-simplified view, akin to a quasi-Marxist class—or intergenerational—struggle between parents and their mid-adolescent children misses a vital point: that mid-adolescents' unconscious wish is for their parents not to sacrifice their own authority or their sense of what is right and wrong, even though they may violently disagree with it. The violence of this intergenerational conflict can also mask the adolescent's intense ambivalence about growing up and the feeling of having been robbed of childhood by time. Indeed, the intergenerational conflict may be the very thing that enables the progressive drive to flourish and prevail over the regressive pull to childhood dependence and all its comforts.

Learning about relationships and sexuality is unavoidably complex and must be grasped as such: every parent will find that something about how they did things in relation to their own parents—present or absent—will inevitably be challenged by how their adolescents act in relation to them as they become sexually active and find a partner, and perhaps even more so if they don't find one. Just as all parents encounter the ghost of their own parents in their rearing of their children—either in gratitude or to their horror—so all parents also encounter themselves as adolescents who are, in turn, in a relationship with their own parents, with whom they identify or from whom they try desperately to be as different as possible. The re-experience by parents of their own adolescence—as their children pass through theirs—is what gives a starting point for parents to be able to help their own adolescents through the challenges to their development posed by technology and the modern world.

What we note about Anna is that in getting pregnant, she possibly hopes to leave behind an unhappy situation and an unhappy history. In so doing, she may possibly be repeating a situation in which she prematurely leaves a family, just as she was prematurely left by her natural father. The empty space created in her mind by this abandonment was temporarily filled by a stepfather, who then did the same thing. Her mother's new partner seems to be failing to fill the gap. Is it possible that James enters Anna's life, but there is a fear that he, too, will leave? Does a baby fill an aching gap more effectively, because a baby is dependent and cannot leave?

These are only possibilities, but the point of considering them is to point to a practical expression of how parents' encounter with their own adolescence in their adolescent child means that there is a period during which the potential adult individual emerging from childhood cannot be expected to function in an autonomous manner. It might be said that Anna "uses" her body and James to express a way of gaining some kind of active control over her history. This is not necessarily to be thought of as a conscious use. She is perhaps using the adult physiological capabilities of her body before she is psychologically able to accept adult responsibilities for her child. This is revealed by her distress at being pregnant.

We can see that mid-adolescence—from 14 to 17 years—is a period that can potentially be complicated in that while it may appear that these adolescents *look* like adults, they may feel inside—without being aware of it consciously—like an uneasy composite of the new and the old. The shock of the new beckoning potentials of adulthood will mingle with the mourning for the departing security or trauma of childhood. It means that that the mid-adolescent may experience other people in the light of this uneasy mix, with the result that nobody feels quite real. Until this sense of "being real"—as Donald Winnicott put it—is achieved, all social interaction has a quality of being a use of the other, and hence making love with another person is not quite possible. In chapter 4 we look at the mid-adolescent's use of identifications and how these are revealed in the youth culture.

4

identity and peer groups: fashion and "youth culture"

We have already seen how young adolescents have to cope with a sense of a new body and how they incorporate this new body into a sense of themselves. This process inevitably alters their relationship with their parents and families. There is a way in which they seem to grow away from their families and want to be as unlike them as they can be. As an expression of this movement, images of adolescent icons abound in the media—often with an apparent intention to shock the older generation.

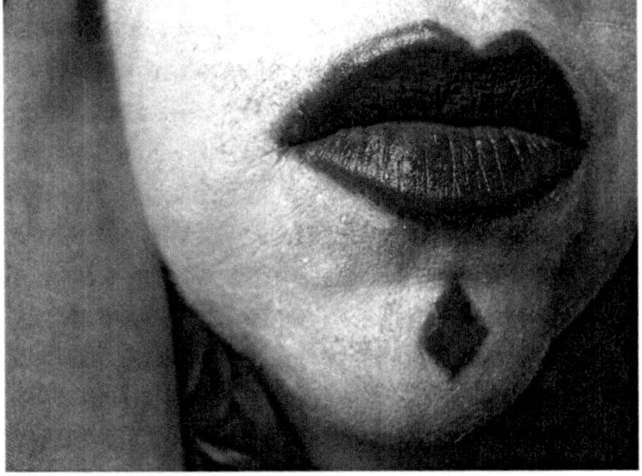

Mohican

Compare the images shown here with the description by Anna Freud of the arrival of adolescence:

> Whereas the latency child (approximately five to eleven, twelve years) had begun to show definite and well-circumscribed character and personality traits, the pre-adolescent (approximately eleven, twelve to fourteen years) is once more unpredictable. Where the latency child has become modest, reasonable and well-mannered with regard to food, the pre-adolescent reacts with greed and demandingness; insatiableness in pre-adolescence frequently leads to thefts of food and sweets. Similar changes occur in almost all the spheres of the child's life. Pre-adolescent boys in particular are known to be dirty in their lavatory habits and negligent in their clothing. Cruel and bullying actions are regular occurrences; so are mutual masturbation, the seduction of younger children, and sexual compliance towards older playmates; destructive acts, thefts and robberies are carried out alone or in company with others. Within the family the preadolescent causes disharmony

> by his selfishness and inconsiderateness; in school he is frequently in trouble because of his lack of interest in the school subjects, his inability to concentrate, his irresponsibleness and insubordination. In short, the whole promising process of adaptation to the environment seems to have stopped short. What parents and teachers are confronted with is *once again* the full, undiminished impact of the instinctual forces within the child. [A. Freud, 1949; emphasis added]

There is no doubt that the activities described by Anna Freud do happen, but opinion is divided about how widespread and important this pattern is. Those who focus more on the sociology of adolescence will say that the majority of adolescents do not in fact display the disturbance described by those who look more at the psychology of adolescence and seek to understand the experience of adolescents as they are going through the process of adolescing.

What does often start to emerge in mid-adolescence is what has come to be known as the adolescent peer group. This group can consist either of a known and identifiable set of individuals with whom the adolescent socializes and spends much time, or a group with whom an adolescent identifies in terms of aspirations and values—in this sense, this kind of "peer group" functions almost like a social class. Some parents might be familiar with the "mods" and "rockers"—the modern equivalent might be the "grungies" or "townies".

Peer groups and a growing sense of identity

The images we see above are almost icons of the "peer group" in the latter sense, but they will in some cases function as totems, bringing together different mid-adolescents and providing a means through which they can identify with one another. Clothes and designer logos provide further means for this. Every parent has experienced the pressure to help their adolescents acquire the "right gear" and will notice the strenuous efforts to refuse conformity, only to replace it with what simply seems to be another uniform, with its own implied conformity.

Thus, we see that another feature of peer groups is what is known as "peer group pressure". In chapter 3 we saw how in some cases this acts as a pressure to violate social norms, but it cannot be said that these groups function in this way in all cases. They often seem to be a means for individual adolescents to find a way of *being with one another* rather than simply *doing things together*. This is a case, perhaps, of "birds of a feather flock together". The adolescent's use of the telephone reflects this difference. A while before the mobile phone became near-universal, some felt that telephoning and being telephoned had become indices of status, popularity, and peer group affiliation, and thus of self-esteem, for adolescents. This is in contrast to children's and adults' use of the telephone, which is to simply pass on or request information for the purpose of doing things together. Today the significance to adolescents of the mobile phone testifies to the importance of this means of communication, which was far less widespread even a decade ago and perhaps accounts in part for the enormous growth in mobile phone theft.

What we can see is that social acceptance, acquired through apparently being accepted by the peer group is, in some ways, similar to the younger adolescents' acceptance of their body. The link is in the experience of acceptance by someone outside the adolescent's immediate control. You cannot control when someone rings you up, any more than you can know what someone really thinks about what you look like. "Hanging out" together is a complex and elaborate experience of the acquisition of an identity of what can, in some cases, be enormous power.

What has been noted is the use of these groups and how they seem to impose a kind of conformity but are very possibly the means through which many adolescents acquire the security to confront differences—particularly the difference from the opposite sex. Thus the peer group apparently imposing conformity seems to be something temporary—but it performs an essential function in helping mid-adolescents to acquire a new identity and to separate from childhood, and, once this is established, giving them the security to expand their social contacts towards those beyond their immediate peer group.

Youth culture and rites of passage

It has often been noted that the transition from childhood to adulthood is mediated in different ways in different societies. Long ago, Margaret Mead (1930) found that growing up in New Guinea was very different from the United States. We have already referred to the different "rites of passage" that must be negotiated by young adolescents on their way to adult status in different societies or religious groups. If these formal institutions are absent, what happens? Could the apparent "storm and struggle" thought by some to be the experience of Western adolescents really be the result of the absence of these formal rituals?

In Western cultures there are, of course, various ages that, once reached, confer new privileges and responsibilities, culminating in an age of majority. We have already noted the different ages of consent for genital sex between the United Kingdom and Holland. We have ages defining criminal responsibility, being able to drive a motor vehicle, being able to buy and consume alcohol in a public house, being able to consent to medical treatment, and being able to join the armed forces. For some reason, different countries have different ages for these, which surely reflects a national attitude to adolescents at different ages and what should be required of them and what can be expected of them. Arguably, these are the nearest that we get to a recognized ritual marking the passage into a more adult status simply as a result of the passage of time since we were born. Some religious groups mark a passage to adulthood with a ceremony or ritual that may or may not be actually carried out—for example, the *bar mitzvah* or *bat mitzvah* of the Jewish faith. Our educational system requires examinations to be taken at particular ages and formal education to be continued until the age of 16. All these mark understandings of the cognitive and social capability of adolescents as they develop and grow towards adulthood.

But how individual adolescents and their families actually experience and pass through this period is something about which it is difficult to generalize, nor can one predict what form it will take for any individual. What we can say is that the arrival of the sexual body at puberty is an irreversible event: there is no going back to childhood, no matter what the individual wishes. We can also have a pretty good idea of the various ways in which any one person might resist this insistence of biology and the way it is recognized by society. We can also say with a fair degree of confidence that because it is an irreversible and inevitable change, there will be a sense of separation from the past and an anxiety about the future, just as there is with all change.

The purpose in saying all this is to suggest that, even if some, taking a sociological view, say that in the case of most adolescents we do not see the disturbed behaviour expected by some psychoanalysts, this does not mean that going through adolescence is not a disturbing experience for most. However, this may simply reflect the extent to which their families and other formal or informal social institutions are able to manage these anxieties. It does not mean that these anxieties are absent or are fabrications of erroneous theory. This is revealed when things go wrong and there is an apparent breakdown in the process of an adolescent's development. It is to these matters that we now turn.

Is disorder and disturbance in mid-adolescence inevitable and normal?

This raises the question of what we are to take as disturbance. Anna Freud took the view that during adolescence a degree of disturbance was normal and to be expected; it would be abnormal if it were not present. But how are we to tell the difference between healthy "normal" disturbance and more worrying manifestations? This is not easy, and what might be merely a passing phase for one individual may be much more threatening for another. The first mistake that can be made is to imagine that this decision can be made quickly. Normal development should be regarded as a process that seems to see-saw between progress and regression. This is inevitable, because progression means giving up the hard-won equilibria of earlier days. Regressive patterns may simply reflect sadness at giving up the older patterns of behaving, relating, and feeling.

We must also make allowances for the fact that the process of adolescent development will be experienced as disturbing to a parent or another adult as that young person passes through stages that had been disturbing for that adult. We cannot expect to be completely flawless and objective observers of the adolescent experience. We saw, looking at the images above, that they can disturb, and indeed may do so—intentionally or not. We are seeing someone deliberately setting out to be different. Passing into or encountering difference means—at some level—separation from familiarity.

Given all these influences hampering our objectivity and capacity to judge when development is going awry, must we conclude that we face an impossible task? Winnicott thought that with adolescents we "play for time". This is not an attitude of "laissez-faire" or one of absent "wait and see": what he asks is that we hold our developing adolescent in mind over a period of time—observing patterns as they develop—so that we do not fall into the trap of not seeing the wood for the trees. This is not easy, because with any one adolescent we—as adults, parents, or professionals—only get the one chance; but we have been through an adolescence ourselves.

Going back to the prisoner's dilemma discussed in chapter 2, we recall that there is a moment when the individual subject can think that he must hasten to declare himself, lest the others recognize themselves for who they are and beat him to it. This rests on the recognition of what the others do not do, as revealed by their inertia. But before this can happen, there has to be a time when the prisoner must identify with the others and experience himself unconsciously as being the same. It is only when he recognizes himself consciously as the same but then realizes that because of their inertia they do not recognize that they are the same, that he recognizes his difference and becomes an individual in his own right. This will all sound very odd until we remember that anyone's perception of another is in part their own creation—not entirely, but at least in part. Out of the identification with the other comes a realization that their experience is not the same as one's own. Thus, the individual as a person in their own right is born.

If we apply the solution of this dilemma to the understanding of adolescence, we might say that the problem for every one of us is to find the means of leaving childhood and entering adulthood, and the means by which we do this is by going through the process of adolescing—all of us in our own idiosyncratic ways. Our new sexual bodies insist that we are different from before and that there are, biologically speaking, only two alternatives, different and complementary to one another—again biologically speaking. Becoming an adult means, however, recognizing not just our gender but our individuality, enabling us to speak as individuals—using the first-person sense of "I"—rather than unconsciously seeing our identity in terms confined to who it is whom we resemble or with whom we identify.

We might think that the function of the peer group as discussed in this chapter is to serve as a group with whom the mid-adolescent can do things—but that is not the point. People who see youth clubs as places to keep restless youth occupied are perhaps missing the point of the peer group. The peer group serves to provide the mid-adolescent with a means of finding a way of being with others. This will mean sorting out his similarities with, and differences from, others. The youth club provides a means for adolescents to find people of their own age but also to meet adults who are not parents or teachers or those exercising authority over them.

Youth workers have the most difficult job of maintaining their own personal authority and blending it with their authority in their role in the various activities of the club. They can thus help adolescents to find their own authority—but they cannot do this for them. Neither should they be expected to attempt to provide role models with whom adolescents can uncritically identify. By the adolescents they will inevitably be seen as adults, and they will be under constant scrutiny to see how they resolve the matter of becoming adults.

In summary, the function of the peer group and its societal representative—"youth culture"—is a complex one. The shock of the arrival of the new sexual body inevitably creates in an individual a feeling of self that is quite different from the earlier feeling of being a child. To become adults in their own right who do not feel inalienably different from all others, individual adolescents must experience and gradually become aware of their identity and sameness with some others in order to brave the encounter with those who are different. This allows the achievement of an adult sense of seeing our individuality in terms of our own similarity with and differences from others and accounts for the puzzling feature of the peer group seeming to enable the discovery of individuality through conformity. The role of the peer group is to facilitate this process, and the mid-adolescent who is not part of such a group is in trouble indeed.

5

psychosocial disturbances

We have already seen that there is a difference in the way adolescents are perceived between those who take a sociological perspective and those who look at the experience from a psychological point of view. Up to now we have taken much more of a psychological approach; it is time to look at the sociological perspective. In the broadest of terms, from this point of view we can see that going through adolescence is a disturbing experience for the individual adolescent, but how this is expressed varies a great deal. What partly determines how it is expressed are the opportunities available, which can be called the causes of psychosocial disturbance.

However, it may be more helpful to think of them not so much as causes but as situations that create opportunities for the emergence of disturbances within individual adolescents. Thus the availability of drugs, the social construction of peer groups, the quality and nature of the educational system, the availability—or lack—of employment provide opportunities for adolescents to express their antisocial tendencies. The fact is that by no means all adolescents take advantage of these opportunities, and only a minority do so to the degree that their behaviour becomes a problem to themselves and to those around them.

This fact by itself will not, however, allay the anxieties of parents, because the increasing independence of adolescents means that fantasies about what they are up to when they are not at home will always be there to some degree. Parents worry about both what is happening now and what might happen. Once something actually does happen, then the situation changes, and this can be responded to; but living in anxiety of what might happen can be much more wearing. It is not difficult to see that parents' anxieties about their adolescent children will be a mixture of their own experience of adolescence, coupled with their understanding of their adolescent, what is going on in the family, and the current social situation in their neighbourhood.

Some facts about adolescent delinquency

If we look at the statistical facts about delinquency, we find that such behaviour reaches a peak in the mid-adolescent period. For example, if we look at the numbers of persons found guilty of, or cautioned for, indictable offences per 100,000 of the population, in England and Wales during 2001, classified by age and gender, we see a clear indication of a trend rising to a peak and then progressively dropping afterwards. It is said that 80% of delinquents stop offending by the age of 17. Girls offend much less frequently than do boys and reach a peak before boys, but the tendency for offending to rise and then fall with age is common and thought to be universal across different cultures (Figure 5.1).

This information tells us nothing, of course, about individuals, but it does suggest something about the conditions in the population as a whole, as well as something about a difference between girls and boys: offending by boys is much more prevalent than by girls, but there is peak during mid-adolescence for both. Some studies have asked adolescents about the kinds of

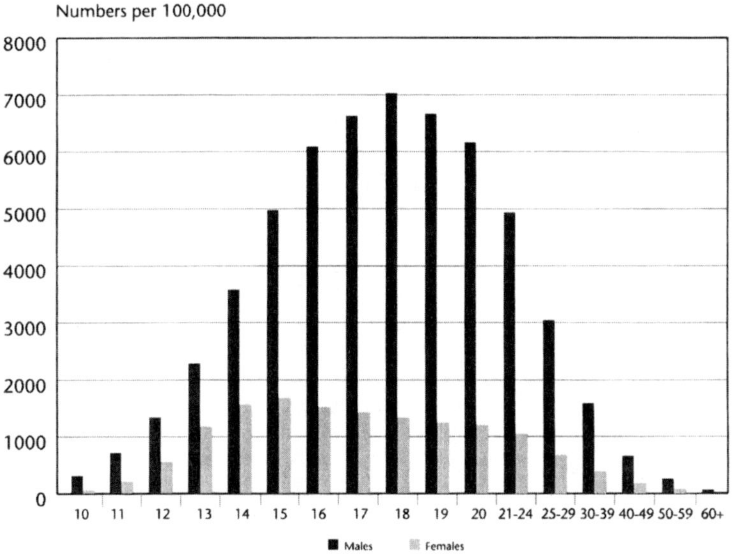

SOURCE: *Criminal Statistics, England and Wales, 2001*. Research, Development & Statistics Directorate and National Statistics. © Crown Copyright 2002.

Figure 5.1. Persons found guilty of, or cautioned for indictable offences per 100,000 population, by age and gender in England and Wales, 2001.

offences they have committed. These self-report studies indicate that 25% of boys and 20% of girls have taken something from a shop and 23% of boys and 7% of girls have carried a weapon. Again these figures increase steadily from school year 7 to 11 (age 12–16).

The most obvious conclusion that can be made is the clear distinction between boys and girls in offending behaviour. But these statistics tell us little about what an individual adolescent may do. The point is twofold: The first is that objective reality as reflected in the statistics and parental anxiety may combine to create an atmosphere of suspicion, and this, in turn, may create a distance between adolescent and parents. This is true for both sexes. The second is the clear peak and fall of offending during the period of mid-adolescence. This suggests something fundamental about this age group (Figure 5.2).

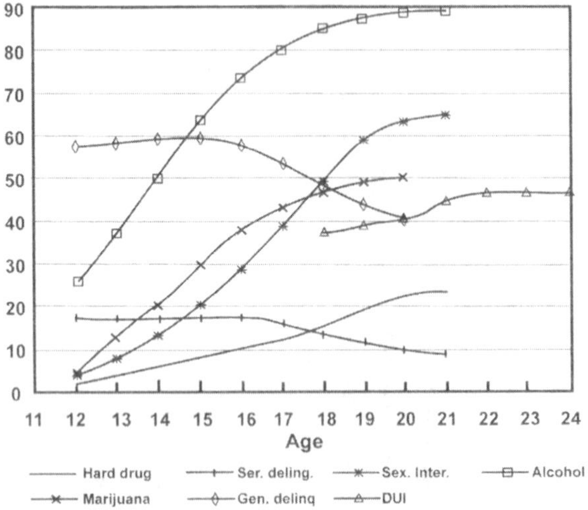

SOURCE: Millstein, Petersen, & Nightingale (1996)

Figure 5.2. Developmental change in problem behaviour.

Another cause of psychosocial disturbance is the availability of drugs and the use of alcohol by adolescents.

In Table 5.1 we can see the peak and fall of delinquency and serious delinquency. The situation with drug use is different in that the rise and fall in use is not observed in the same obvious way. It seems more likely that the individual develops a particular trend, and this continues almost as if some kind of choice has been made—consciously or unconsciously. To understand this situation, we probably need to look at the prevailing social norms and the individual's social situation: specifically, the family and the peer group. Thus we see a clear increase in the use of alcohol and marijuana—the readily available and socially acceptable drugs—and a slower increase and much less prevalent use of hard drugs. Nevertheless, in contrast to delinquency, there is an increase, which is probably due to the fact that the behaviour itself is less likely to have a direct impact on other people. A social response is therefore less likely, despite the fact that Class A drug use is illegal. This

Table 5.1. Prevalence (in percentages) of self-reported offending, by age and gender, 2001

	Year 7		*Year 8*		*Year 9*		*Year 10*		*Year 11*	
	boys	*girls*	*boys*	*girls*	*boys*	*girls*	*boys*	*girls*	*boys*	*girls*
Ever stolen anything?	23.2	16.6	31.5	25.2	39.2	36.2	44.0	39.2	43.9	37.4
Shoplifted in last year?	11.4	6.8	18.3	16.6	23.0	24.1	27.6	25.7	25.7	20.3
Stolen/tried to steal a vehicle in last year?	1.1	0.1	2.9	1.0	4.9	0.8	5.9	2.3	7.2	2.0
Stolen/tried to steal from vehicle in last year?	1.4	0.8	3.9	1.0	4.3	1.0	6.1	2.2	6.9	2.0
Stolen/tried to steal something else in last year?	12.7	7.1	15.8	10.2	20.6	14.7	23.3	15.1	18.7	11.1
Broken into building intending to steal in last year?	2.2	0.8	4.8	2.1	6.6	1.6	8.8	3.5	9.7	3.6
Vandalized property in last year?	13.4	8.8	19.3	18.5	24.8	24.2	30.8	32.9	30.0	25.0
Handled stolen food in last year?	7.2	4.4	17.9	11.7	22.1	16.1	28.9	21.6	28.3	18.9
Attacked someone intending harm in last year?	7.8	3.4	13.8	7.4	17.0	7.0	17.3	9	18.9	8.5
Carried weapon in last year?	10.4	2.1	17.8	4.5	20.1	5.0	22.8	6.5	23.6	7.8
Ever sold/dealt drugs?	1.0	0.1	2.6	0.9	4.0	1.9	7.5	6.2	11	5.5
Ever been arrested?	4.2	0.9	7.9	3.7	11.4	4.1	14.8	6.4	13.2	6.8

Source: *Risk and Protective Factors Associated with Youth Crime and Effective Interventions to Prevent It*. Youth Justice Board, 2001.

is not to say that drug use has no indirect effect on other people. The link between drug use and other forms of crime has been well established.

The universal age–crime curve

Nevertheless, one of the most extraordinary features of the so-called age–crime curve is its universality. The general pattern of crime rising to a peak and then falling is seen in different countries and cultures. Gottfredson and Hirshi (1990) showed that the age–crime curve in England and Wales was much the same in 1842–44, in 1903, and in 1965. The other feature is the gender difference showing that boys are much more likely to offend than are girls. David Farrington (1986) has provided some evidence to suggest that the age at which crime peaks has risen in the last 60 years—possibly related to the raising of the school-leaving age. Thus in 1938 crime peaked at age 13, in 1961 at 14, and in 1983 at age 15.

Whether the increase truly reflects an actual increase in delinquency has been questioned. Rutter and Giller (1983) said:

> Of course official statistics show that delinquency reaches a peak during the middle or late teens, with many individuals not receiving their first conviction until well into adolescence or even early adult life. But this simply reflects the fact that, by law, young children cannot be convicted, that the police are less likely to prosecute young first offenders and that it may take some time for delinquent activities to be detected. Certainly both self-report data and behavioural ratings from teachers and others make clear that most delinquent individuals already show some form of antisocial behaviour during middle childhood or pre-adolescence.

This suggests that a child's antisocial behaviour becomes more and more noticeable as the child gets older and less and less tolerable by society. As an example of how this can even affect research methods, according to David Farrington, it was found in a study of the difference between offenders and non-offenders in London that 96% of inner-city London males admitted to committing at least one of ten common offences (including theft, burglary, violence, vandalism, and drug abuse) at some time between the ages of 10 and 32, but only 33% had been convicted of at least one of these offences during this age range. "In order to compare offenders and non-offenders, it is important to set a sufficiently high criterion for 'offending' . . . so that the vast majority of the male population are not classified as offenders."

What is really difficult to account for is the fall in the incidence in crime. This is not to say that the overall incidence of crime has not increased during the last century: it has done so. But some individuals do decide to give up crime—and why this is so is not yet clearly understood. Even to begin, we need to shift the focus to thinking about individual experience, but making the jump from what we can learn from statistics derived from populations to thinking about individuals is not easy and is inherently unreliable. All that we can really hope for are directions.

When we do shift the focus from looking at the relation between age and crime and how it is affected by factors such as social class to taking a more person-oriented approach, a rather different perspective emerges. A study in Sweden (Magnusson & Bergman, 1988) of the development of antisocial behaviour in boys over a significant period of time found that at the age of 13, risk factors such as aggressiveness, poor concentration, and underachievement were closely related to outcomes such as crime, drug abuse, and psychiatric illness up to age 23. Single risk factors, such as aggressiveness, significantly predicted single outcomes, such as crime and alcohol abuse. But when the 13% of boys with multiple risk factors were excluded, these significant relationships disappeared. This suggests that many of the results obtained in studies relating the incidence of crime to age in a population might be produced by a minority of chronically antisocial people.

There are two conclusions that we should not draw from this. The first might be that we can safely assume that the antisocial tendency is confined to a small group. Following from this, we might come to the conclusion that most young people do not experience whatever it is that leads the chronically antisocial to do what they do. As we saw above, 96% of inner-city London males admitted to committing an offence, but only 33% were convicted. Would it be more accurate to say "boasted about" rather than "admitted"? Were they telling the truth, and how would we know? And what of the "crime"? Can we really equate smoking a joint with a robbery with violence? As we noticed above, the use of drugs does not follow the same pattern as that of the age–crime curve, perhaps because the direct impact of drug use on society is not as obvious as is that of violence. Indirectly, of course, drugs usage does impact on society because of the link between drugs and violence to obtain the means to support their use.

The antisocial tendency

But a conclusion that we can draw that might be a little more useful to the parent of the individual adolescent is that while the expression of an antisocial tendency is sometimes obvious, at other times it is not seen because it is contained, without adolescents or their parents being very aware of it. This means that such a tendency does not come to the surface because the environment—social or physical—is sufficiently robust to absorb the batterings of the tendency without being in any way remarkable. Furthermore, it may be that society creates places where the tendency can be expressed in an unremarkable way because the adult world colludes with it.

To think about this, we need to consider the tendency to be antisocial in terms broader than simply its behavioural expression. Donald Winnicott (1956) saw a link between the antisocial tendency and deprivation. This was a long time ago now, and it is interesting how his thoughts seem to have been very largely forgotten. A recent review (Farrington, 1995) of "what is known about teenage antisocial behaviour" makes no mention of Winnicott at all. He was, of course, writing a decade after the end of the Second World War, and he felt that the greatest expression of the adult world's hatred of their adolescents had been in sending millions of young men—in the main, late adolescents, not even young adults—to their deaths in that war. He was perhaps writing about deprivation in acknowledgement of that fact, the shadow of which has

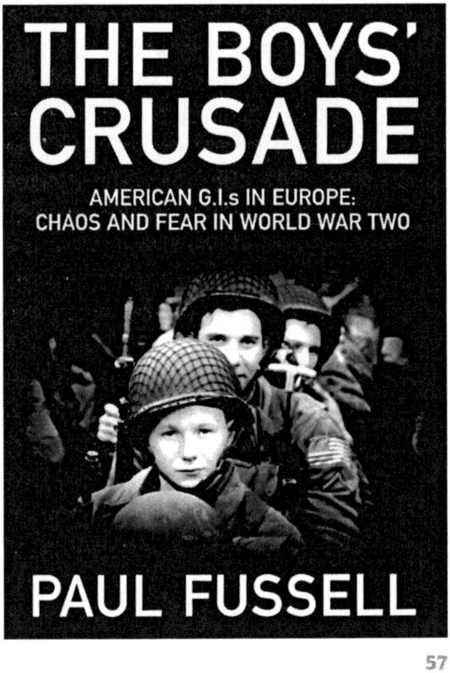

Photograph courtesy of the Imperial War Museum, London

receded with the passage of time, only now to be replaced by other shadows.

But what did Winnicott (1956) mean by the antisocial tendency, and how did he see it expressed? Perhaps the following story will give us a flavour:

> I was asked by a friend to discuss the case of her son, the eldest of a family of four. She could not bring John to me in an open way because of her husband who objects to psychology on religious grounds. All she could do was to have a talk with me about the boy's compulsion to steal, which was developing into something quite serious; he was stealing in a big way from shops as well as at home. It was not possible for practical reasons to arrange for anything else but for the mother and myself to have a quick meal together in a restaurant, in the course of which she told me about the troubles and asked me for advice. There was nothing for me to do unless I could do it then and there. I therefore explained the meaning of the stealing and suggested that she should find a good moment in her relationship with the boy and make an interpretation to him. It appeared that she and John had a good relationship with each other for a few moments each evening after he had gone to bed; usually at such a time he would discuss the stars and the moon. This moment could be used.
>
> I said: "Why not tell him that you know that when he steals he is not wanting the things that he steals but he is looking for something that he has a right to: that he is making a claim on his mother and father because he feels deprived of their love." I told her to use language which he could understand. I may say that I knew enough of this family, in which both the parents are musicians, to see how it was that this boy had become to some extent a deprived child, although he has a good home.
>
> Some time later I had a letter telling me that she had done what I suggested. She wrote: "I told him that what he

> really wanted when he stole money and food and things was his mum; and I must say I didn't really expect him to understand, but he did seem to. I asked him if he thought we didn't love him because he was so naughty sometimes, and he said right out that he didn't think we did, much. Poor little scrap! I felt so awful, I can't tell you. So I told him never, never to doubt it again and if he ever did feel doubtful to remind me to tell him again. But of course I shan't need reminding for a long time, it's been such a shock. One seems to need these shocks. So I'm being a lot more demonstrative to try and keep him from being doubtful any more. And up to now there's been absolutely no more stealing."
>
> The mother had had a talk with the form teacher and had explained to her that the boy was in need of love and appreciation, and had gained her co-operation although the boy gives a lot of trouble at school.
>
> Now after eight months it is possible to report that there has been no return of stealing, and the relationship between the boy and his family has very much improved.
>
> In considering this case it must be remembered that I had known the mother very well during her adolescence and to some extent had seen her through an antisocial phase of her own. She was the eldest in a large family. She had a very good home but very strong discipline was exerted by the father, especially at the time when she was a small child. What I did therefore had the effect of a double therapy, enabling this young woman to get insight into her own difficulties through the help that she was able to give to her son. When we are able to help parents to help their children we do in fact help them about themselves. [Winnicott, 1956, pp. 307–308]

We can see from this story that Winnicott saw the antisocial tendency—typically characterized by stealing and lying—as an attempt to get back something that the boy felt had been taken from him. Hence the reference to *deprivation* and not straightforward *privation*—that is, *something that the adolescent had never had.* For Winnicott, the child who steals an object is looking not for the stolen object but for the mother over whom he or she has rights. These rights derive from the fact that (from the child's point of view) the mother was created by the child.

This may seem a very odd idea, but if we accept that what we perceive of the world is not purely neutrally objective but is heavily infused with our own wishes, then it becomes a little clearer. It means that the mother we come to know from the day we were born comes to be a creation made up of the totality of our experience of her, with all its happinesses, gratifications, frustrations, and sadnesses. By this means, she becomes part of our life and our self. If, for any reason, we feel we are deprived of her in any way, then, Winnicott suggests, we seek and find her and express this searching and finding by stealing.

But there is another side to the antisocial tendency, which is destructiveness, sometimes expressed by lying, but also in other ways, such as making a mess. In general terms, Winnicott felt that the child is looking for an environmental stability that will withstand and survive the strain resulting from impulsive behaviour. This is often referred to as "testing a boundary" and will perhaps be very familiar to parents in the battles over at what time their adolescent children are expected to be home at night.

Another expression of the mess-making is the adolescent bedroom and the seemingly endless failure to get young people to put their dirty clothes into the washing and to clean up after they've finished doing something. It can all look very regressive, particularly after "they seemed to be so good when they were younger". It can also seem very aggressive towards parents and generate a lot of hateful feelings and angry outbursts on both sides, to the point where it seems that neither parent nor adolescent can stand one another—or, indeed, ever will. The most extraordinary thing that Winnicott then suggests is that *the antisocial tendency is an expression of hope.* How can it be, that all this destructiveness we see is an expression of hope when it all seems so pointless? And don't modern youth have more privileges and opportunities than we ever had in our day? Aren't they simply just spoilt brats?

No matter how preposterous Winnicott's idea seems to be, it does help us to develop an idea about why the age–crime curve takes the shape that it does. It also gives us a chance to think again about what happens with the arrival of puberty. The first characteristic we might notice about the antisocial tendency is that it seems paradoxical to regard stealing as the search for a lost loved object. This is further complicated by the fact that the "antisocial" adolescent seems to treat loved ones apparently very badly. We have a peculiar situation in that the adolescent's love seems to be expressed in ways that can seem very hateful to those on the receiving end. No wonder parents sometimes feel they can't understand their adolescent children, and their children sometimes don't feel understood.

The antisocial tendency and the sense of the future

So why should this paradoxical behaviour be an expression of hope? The point is that you don't search unless you hope to find. The search is an expression of a feeling about the future. But, then, why should adolescents feel that they have lost anything? If we think that with the arrival of puberty comes a feeling of change and that life will never be the same again, it will follow that with this sense of change comes an inevitable sense of loss, mingled with the pleasurable but possibly intimidating shock of the new. But the sense of loss is always there, and the batterings on the old family boundaries represent a desire to leave and break free, with the reassuring feeling that the family will not be damaged by the adolescent's departure and be still there on their return.

Turning now to the age–crime curve, we have seen that its most universal quality is refraining from crime from the late teens and early twenties onward. We have also noted that the age at which the tendency seems to peak seemed to rise in accordance with the raising of the school leaving age. If we think of the paradoxical pattern of the adolescent being hateful to those loved, we might be reminded of Juliet's predicament created by her love for Romeo. If she is to leave the family and find a partner appropriate to her adult status, she will choose a partner who is in some way inimical to her parents. When I use the word "will" here, I do not mean it to signify necessarily a conscious choice. Her parents may—in actual fact—be delighted, but because for her the choice implies the breaking of her dependent infantile ties to her parents, her reluctance to do this will be expressed by perceiving them as the ones who are resistant, not herself: to be conscious of her own resistance would threaten to maintain these dependent ties.

Of course, if her parents are not, in fact, delighted, it may be that they are reluctant to let their daughter become an adult and cannot face the fact of their certain displacement by a new generation and its implication of their death. In Shakespeare's "*Romeo and Juliet*" this is expressed by the parents' choice of a partner for Juliet and her father's rather dictatorial attitude in his insistence upon his daughter's marriage to someone she does not love.

We are therefore led to the idea that something stable, predictable, and familiar is undone with the arrival of puberty, both in the experience of adolescents and in how they are experienced by their parents, families, and those immediately around them. The latency—or pre-pubertal—child, who had once given the parents so much hope, can seem to have changed into the "enemy within". Much antisocial behaviour is not recorded in the official statistics as it rises to its apparent peak, possibly because the world finds a way of absorbing the majority of it. Then, once the peak is passed, there is a predictable reduction in disturbance as whatever was undone seems to find a way of doing up again. It is possible that what we see in the population, reflected in the official statistics, is repeated in the individual adolescent but expressed in their own unique way reflecting their histories and the environment in which they find themselves.

The question is: what is this *something* that undoes and seems to do up again? To get a view on this, we might now ask what happens if the undoing does not seem to mend spontaneously. We have considered the adolescent who becomes behaviourally disturbed. To learn more about this something, let us now think about the adolescent who becomes emotionally disturbed, and how that may be expressed.

6

emotional disturbance

In chapter 5 we saw that the frequency of delinquency seems to rise to a peak during the mid-teens and then begins to drop. What was also clear from the statistics was the gender difference, in that males seem much more likely to offend than do females. In this chapter we think about the frequency of mental disturbance as it appears in the general population, to see whether we can learn something about the kinds of emotional difficulties young people of this age can experience.

When it comes to thinking about emotional disturbance, we tend to think of signs other than offending. It seems clear that this does cause emotional disturbance as well as being caused by it. However, apart from offending, it is depression, self-harming, and suicide that seem to be the most worrying signs that a mid-adolescent is feeling disturbed. Here, again, we find a gender difference.

In Table 6.1 we can see that there is an enormous increase in the rate of suicide and unexplained death in the 15–24 age group, compared to those 14 years old and younger. Furthermore, the numbers and rate of increase are far greater for boys than for girls.

The situation is reversed, however, when we look at deliberate self-harm and thinking about suicide as opposed to doing it. A survey carried out for the Samaritans (Hawton, Fagg,

Table 6.1. Number of suicides and undetermined deaths in the UK, by age and gender

	1991	*1995*	*2000*
Male			
0–14	18	17	21
15–24	731	601	555
25–34	1,031	1,154	1,037
Female			
0–14	4	15	11
15–24	142	139	143
25–34	263	242	258

Source: Office for National Statistics, General Register Office for Scotland, General Register Office for Northern Ireland, Central Statistics Office Ireland.

Simkin, Bate, & Bond, 2000) asked 6,000 young people about whether they had deliberately self-harmed or thought about suicide during the previous year. Findings from this survey show that young women seem to be nearly four times more likely to self-harm. Furthermore, whereas boys are four times more likely actually to kill themselves, girls, who do not self-harm, are nearly three times more likely to think about suicide than are boys (Table 6.2).

If we now look at other forms of mental illness, we find that a pattern seems to distinguish males from females, and this pattern seems to extend well into adult life: more females experience depression or generalized anxiety than do males, but there is no difference between the genders in their propensity to experience panic disorders or experience obsessive compulsions to do something (Table 6.3).

Table 6.2. Prevalence of deliberate self-harm and suicidal ideation in previous year, based on descriptions provided by adolescents

	No. of respondents	*Self harm/suicidal ideation*	
		no.	*(%)*
Deliberate self-harm			
males	3,478	98	(3.2)
females	2,703	299	(11.2)
all*	5,801	398	(6.9)
Suicidal ideation (no self-harm)			
males	3,025	258	(8.5)
females	2,692	602	(22.4)
all	5,737	863	(15.4)
No self-harm or suicidal thoughts			
males	3,025	2,669	(88.2)
females	2,692	1,791	(66.5)
all*	5,737	4,476	(78.0)

*Twenty people did not indicate gender.
Source: Hawton et al. (2002).

The internal worlds of adolescent girls and boys

This tells us something about how to interpret these statistical differences observed between boys and girls. Baldly speaking, what the statistics mean is that when we consider boys and girls in separate categories, any difference observed between them means that boys are more or less likely to display a particular kind of behaviour and girls another. Working out how this applies to understanding the individual is difficult to specify, but we can make hypotheses, particularly when the observed differences seem significantly large.

Table 6.3. Prevalence of neurotic disorders, by age and gender

	16–19	*20–24*	*25–29*	*30–34*	*35–39*	*40–44*
Females						
mixed anxiety and depressive disorder	124	138	131	115	92	127
generalized anxiety disorder	11	18	48	39	54	64
depressive episode	27	35	21	30	39	26
all phobias	21	15	26	22	35	30
obsessive compulsive disorder	9	18	16	13	18	18
panic disorder	6	—	12	6	6	5
any neurotic disorder	**192**	**209**	**216**	**205**	**191**	**229**
base	*151*	*258*	*398*	*574*	*564*	*460*
Males						
mixed anxiety and depressive disorder	51	44	93	59	85	89
generalized anxiety disorder	16	11	32	52	53	58
depressive episode	9	8	27	12	36	30
all phobias	6	19	11	18	17	12
obsessive compulsive disorder	9	20	8	8	8	9
panic disorder	5	8	8	8	5	5
any neurotic disorder	**86**	**100**	**152**	**130**	**154**	**162**
base	*183*	*202*	*332*	*379*	*442*	*382*

*People may have more than one type of disorder.
Source: Singleton et al. (2001).

These figures give an impression that girls are more likely to have a sense of experiencing themselves from within themselves, whereas boys concentrate on how they seem to be engaging with the world around them. When we were thinking earlier about emotional and cognitive development during mid-adolescence, there was a clear sense that giving up an egocentric stance towards the world paved the way to a new approach to thinking about the self and the other person. Values and morals become conscious in a new way precisely because of how mid-adolescents see themselves in the world of others. For this reason, identification with those like one becomes a means of feeling safer in the encounter with the *different other*. These figures take us a little further in that we can now see that whereas girls seem to have a sense of experience within themselves, boys seem to be much more inclined to act and, in so doing, to use their bodies. The mediating capacity to reflect and think between the experience of impulse and the resultant action is attenuated for boys. Thus, boys seem to be more at risk from themselves.

If we now look at what young adolescents say they worry about, we can see that boys and girls worry about similar things, but there are some important differences. Overall, girls seem to worry more than boys, which fits the pattern of girls worrying—or "experiencing themselves from within"—while boys often express their anxieties through action (Table 6.4).

From this it seems that girls are more likely to worry—in a way that boys do less—about relationships and themselves in relationships. Girls also seem more likely to worry more than boys about puberty, growing up, and their health, particularly when they would be going through the period of change. After that, they worry about how they look. When asked about HIV/AIDS, girls and boys do not seem to differ very much, which is intriguing because both sexes face the same disease as something in external reality.

Table 6.4. Proportions (in percentages) of 10- to15-year-olds responding "A lot/Quite a lot" to the question: "How much do you worry about these problems?"

	Males			*Females*		
	10–11	*12–13*	*14–15*	*10–11*	*12–13*	*14–15*
School problems	16	22	29	16	22	39
Health problems	20	20	17	23	27	28
Career problems	*	20	28	*	18	36
Problems with friends	*	17	15	*	33	33
Family problems	23	22	24	28	33	41
The way you look	15	23	24	28	45	55
HIV/AIDS	*	11	13	*	13	16
Puberty and growing up	13	15	11	27	25	16
The environment	20	*	*	20		*
None of these	47	45	39	39	28	19

*Options not available.
Source: Balding (2002).

All this suggests that there is something somehow different between the ways boys and girls experience themselves in relation to others in the world around them. Perhaps the boys' predilection for action suggests that they will experience their problems as there being something wrong with the world. Girls, on the other hand, will experience their problems as being somehow within them or that there is something wrong with them.

It seems to make sense that the different experiences that boys and girls have of their bodies as they go through puberty may have something to do with the girls' greater sense of internality. The monthly cycle of the girl's body, once periods are established—sometimes known as the "curse"—is outside boys' direct experience. Boys, because of their accent on action, seem more concerned *about what they will be prevented from doing*. Hence, "mind your own business", "leave me alone" or "what are you looking at?" are common complaints. Girls, on the other hand, seem to be more worried *about what they will not be able to do* or whether they will be chosen.

Once upon a time, "active" was associated with masculine and "passive" with feminine. Experience at the Brandon Centre shows that both boys and girls can seem to be rather careless about contraception in early- to mid-adolescence, behaving as if it "won't happen to me". However, we discovered recently that this apparently casual attitude immediately disappears in girls when they are faced with the loss of their fertility as a result of contracting Chlamydia. Not only do they actively seek treatment to protect their fertility, but they also seek out their partners to ensure that they also receive treatment. We see therefore girls very actively protecting their internal world in the physiological sense as well as in their internal mental preoccupations.

The stranger and complementarity with the other

At the end of chapter 5 it was suggested that with the arrival of puberty something stable, predictable, and familiar is undone—both in the adolescents' own experience and in how they are experienced by their parents, families, and those immediately around them. By looking at the kinds of emotional disturbances experienced by girls and boys, we seem to arrive at a hypothesis that boys express their disturbance through what they do, whereas for girls it is all about how they feel about themselves and others. If this has something to do with how their bodies feel to them as they go through puberty, the conclusion might be that what undoes is something linking the capacity to act with the capacity to experience, think, and reflect on their actions and its consequences for themselves and others. The fact that delinquency and other forms of antisocial behaviour decline as the adolescent progresses towards adulthood suggests that what has been undone does up again.

D. H. Lawrence suggested that adolescence was the time of "the stranger". We seem to find that boys and girls have a different experience of this stranger and consequently relate to their peers in a different way. Puberty brings an awareness of the other sex that is new and gives a sense that "life will never be the same again". We have also noted that there is a rise in the antisocial tendency in both boys and girls, and, following Winnicott's hypothesis, we might wonder whether the loss that is being reacted to by the undoing of the link between the capacity to act and the capacity to reflect is the loss of childhood. Adolescents of both sexes face a certain loss of the past and an uncertain future. The travails of mid-adolescence seem to reflect the struggle of each adolescent with this predicament. Not all will experience this struggle as overwhelming, but that depends a great deal on the support of those around them.

In the midst of this struggle, which is to be experienced as a disturbance both for adolescents and for those around them, it is often difficult for parents to see their relevance to the adolescent at a time when their adolescent children seem to treat them as if they are totally irrelevant. There will be times when a parent's anger with an adolescent child will lead to thoughts of abandoning them to their fate. In these moments, it is not easy to see that the source of the provocation is the fear of the loss of childhood and the implied dependency on parents, which the adolescent refuses to acknowledge. For the adolescent that means facing the humiliation of admitting how much they fear the future and believe that they will not be good enough.

If these thoughts give us some idea of the reasons for the undoing that we seem to observe, we must now turn to what it is that enables what has been undone to be mended again. One of the ways in which this undoing is displayed is by adolescent giving to all around the appearance of having fallen into an unrealistic belief of being able to do anything; another way can be an apparent collapse into a helpless withdrawal, from which there seems no return.

The development of two capacities seems to counteract these seeming regressions: the capacity to feel "real" and the capacity to be alone. These lead to being able to recognize one's complementarity with the "other"—a development from the dependency one has experienced as a child. Inevitably, one is dependent on one's parents, but feeling one's complementarity with the "other" means realizing that you need each other and your differences with the other in fact complement one another. This is, in a way, the task of late adolescence. It culminates with becoming an adult, but it begins in mid-adolescence. It is to this that we now turn.

7

on being—and being allowed to be—immature

In the first chapter of this book, Donald Winnicott was quoted as saying:

> What I am writing here (dogmatically in order to be brief) is that the adolescent is immature. Immaturity is an essential element of health at adolescence. There is only one cure for immaturity and that is the passage of time and the growth into maturity that time may bring.
>
> Immaturity is a precious part of the adolescent scene. In this is contained the most exciting features of creative thought, new and fresh feeling, ideas for new living. Society needs to be shaken by the aspirations of those who are not responsible. If the adults abdicate, the adolescent becomes prematurely, and by false process, adult. Advice to society could be: for the sake of adolescents, and of their immaturity, do not allow them to step up and attain a false maturity by handing over to them a responsibility that is not yet theirs, even though they may fight for it. [Winnicott, 1968]

These words can easily be misunderstood, and this usually happens because of the mindset of the reader. When Winnicott says that there is only one cure for immaturity, he might be thought to mean that we must accept that we cannot intervene in or accelerate a process, which will proceed in its own time. The metaphor of laying down wine in the cellar and leaving it to mature undisturbed might come to mind.

But I think he means much more than this, because he speaks to a reader who is an intrinsic part of the maturation process. He insists that the adult cannot abdicate this responsibility, and when he says that "Society needs to be shaken by the aspirations of those who are not responsible", he means that society must go on being responsible. The problem, then, is how this is to be achieved when there seems to be no way of intervening in the adolescent process. He seems to be asking adults to be actively passive. To think of it as adopting a stance of resolute but unobtrusive authoritative presence might be a closer approximation, because the absence of the adult authority gives the adolescent no option but to venture into an authority vacuum before being ready to do so.

Another way of putting this might be to suggest that just as there is no baby without a mother (or father), so there is no adolescent without adult parents, be they present or absent to the external observer. The difference for the adolescent is that they have a sense of what they once were and what they might become. A mother creates a place within which the baby can thrive and be protected from the world. Adults need to create a place within which the adolescent can thrive and from which the adolescent can initially encounter and gradually move into the world. The role of adults, however, is not just to be there protecting their children, but also *to be available to be shaken,* because it is through this that adolescents discover the strength of their own authority. As we see further on, in situations where one of the adolescent's parents is physically absent in a concrete day-to day-way, that parent is rarely absent from the mind of the adolescent child. This psychological fact may be stoutly denied by the adolescent—but the effects of the absent parent are often clear for all to see—provided they look.

An adolescent's view of maturity: the case of Holden Caulfield

In practical terms, we might describe the adult as being asked to walk a tightrope between facilitation and control.

J. D. Salinger's novel *The Catcher in the Rye* (1951) captures many of these dilemmas through the eyes of its hero, Holden Caulfield, and the eyes of those around him. On the matter of maturity, there is the point in the novel when Holden is being advised by his former teacher, Mr Antolini.

> "Oddly enough, this wasn't written by a practicing poet. It was written by a psychoanalyst named Wilhelm Stekel. Here's what he . . .—Are you still with me?"
>
> "Yes, sure I am."
>
> "Here's what he said: 'The mark of the immature man is that he wants to die nobly for a cause, while the mark of the mature man is that he wants to live humbly for one.'"
>
> . . . Boy, I felt so damn *tired* all of a sudden. [p. 195]

This well-meant advice, which apparently makes Holden "so damn tired", contrasts with an earlier passage, in which the meaning of the novel's title is explained. Holden is talking to his sister Phoebe about what he wants to be, shortly after telling her that he has confirmed that he has just been thrown out of school. We might surmise that to be thrown out of school is a metaphor for being forced into the adult world—rather like falling over a cliff—by the imperative of time and age, and so in this passage we see something of Holden's resistance to the fact of growing up. Shortly before the passage that follows, to hide the fact of his being expelled, Holden explains to his sister that he has got out of school early—but then she guesses the truth. Indeed, as we will see, Phoebe, even though she is younger, is portrayed to be somewhat more knowledgeable than Holden, perhaps to capture Holden's fear of adulthood and its requirement of maturity.

Here Holden is speaking:

> "You what I'd like to be?", I said. "You know what I'd like to be? I mean if I had my goddam choice?"
>
> . . . . . .
>
> Anyway, I keep picturing all these little kids playing some game in this big field of rye and all. Thousands of little kids, and nobody'd be around—nobody big, I mean—except me. And I'm standing on the edge of some crazy cliff. What I have to do, I have to catch somebody if they start to go over the cliff—I mean if they're running and they don't look where they are going. I have to come out from somewhere and catch them. That's all I do all day. I'd just be the catcher in the rye and all. I know it's crazy, but that's the only thing I'd really like to be. I know it's crazy."
>
> Old Phoebe didn't say anything for a long time. Then when she said something, all she said was, "Daddy's going to kill you". [p. 179]

Clearly, something in Holden wants to stop him growing up. Shortly before this passage we get a glimpse of what it is that he apparently fears. He is talking to his sister about being a lawyer—his father's profession:

> "And besides, even if you did go around saving guys' lives and all, how would you know if you did it because you really *wanted* to save guys' lives, or you did it because what you *really* wanted to do was be a terrific lawyer, with everybody slapping you on the back. . . . How would you know you weren't being a phoney? The trouble is you wouldn't".

Holden indicates that it is a problem of seeking to do something because of how it appears to others—for him, this condemns one to being phoney. Thus he implies that for him to feel real, he must be in touch with what he wants, not what other people want for him. His trouble, as we learn, is that what he wants to avoid is to fall into adulthood before he feels ready.

But listening to Holden with adult ears, we may find ourselves less than understanding. We may find that we place ourselves into the position of a daddy who wants to kill him. Certainly, Holden can seem to be a quite infuriating adolescent, with his resolute determination to refuse to do what is asked of him when to the adult mind it is obvious that it is in his interest to do it. We get the sense that it is largely because we see it like this that he resists so stiffly.

Reaching for maturity with the encounter with the adult world

Another novel, also written during the post-war years, seeks to capture the essence of this time of immaturity. Colette's *Le Blé en Herbe*[1] describes two adolescents—Phillipe and Vinca—16 and 15 years old, respectively. They have known each other since childhood, and each year their families have gone to the same place on the Brittany coast for their summer holiday. The novel is about the last few weeks of the summer holiday before their return to Paris with their parents.

Having grown up together, "their entire childhoods bound them together, adolescence pulled them apart". The reader is aware of the impending sense that this time the return to Paris will be different, because the relationship between Phillipe and Vinca will have changed forever. Inseparable as children, fishing and swimming throughout the endless holiday days of previous summers, there is a sense that these two have been seen by their parents as destined to marry and bring children into a world of their own. But the growing sense of the changes in their bodies and their consciousness of their looks and appearance seem portents of an entry into a new world of adulthood from which there is no turning away. The summer holidays are no doubt a metaphor for adolescence and the inevitability of the ending, to be followed inexorably by adulthood. What intrudes into Phillipe's gradually fading idyll is the arrival on the scene of Camille Dalleray—initially Madame Dalleray.

As readers, we observe the impact of Camille Dalleray upon Phillipe, which is like a kind of seduction by the older woman. This seduction is all implied and understated, but the attraction of a female stranger draws Phillipe away from his childhood sweetheart and his parents' marital ambitions for him. He feels a terrible sense of responsibility for Vinca. What we know of the seduction is gained simply by implication. Mme. Dalleray's dealings with Phillipe change from those between an adult married woman and a child to one where she addresses him as "Monsieur Phil". This, then, is not a seduction that can be described though the details of a physical sexual encounter—rather, Phillipe is being introduced to the world of adult sexual dealings, to the essential complementarity of men and women. It is a move from a world where parents nurture dependent children to an adult world where differences between individuals complement one another interdependently:

> "Your parents are well, Monsieur Phil?"
>
> He looked at her, surprised. She seemed distracted and appeared not to have heard her own voice. His shirt cuff caught a spoon and it fell, ringing feebly as it hit the rug.
>
> "Clumsy. . . . *Wait* a second "
>
> With one hand she grabbed his fist, and with the other hand she rolled Phil's sleeve up to the elbow and firmly held the naked arm in her warm hand.

> "Let me go!" shouted Phil.
>
> He yanked his hand away violently. A saucer broke at his feet. In the buzzing in his ears he heard the echo of Vinca's cry: "Let go!" and he looked at Madame Dalleray with his eyes full of wrath and questions.
>
> She hadn't budged and the hand he had pulled back lay open on his knees like the hollow of a conch.
>
> For a long time Philippe weighed the meaning of his inability to move. He lowered his head, saw pass before his eyes two or three incoherent, ineluctable images of flight, as one flies in a dream, or of falling, as one falls in diving, at the instant when the folds of the wave are going to join with the face heading toward them—then, without rushing, with a reflective slowness, with a calculated courage, he placed his naked arm back in the open hand.

Throughout the novel we get a feeling of Phillipe's gradual anticipation of what the future holds for him: education and the baccalaureate, military service, then a profession. He feels surrounded by the implicit parental expectation that he and Vinca will marry. We never really discover—and this is the power of the novel—whether these anticipations are entirely his own or are an edifice subtly built from his own desires intertwining with the desires of those around him. The main subjective focus of the novel is Phillipe, but the reader is invited to observe him as he goes through a transition in his feelings about Vinca and in particular how he sees her.

To which one must add, and how she sees him: Vinca, it is slowly revealed, is acutely aware of the changes going on within Phillipe. She also realizes that something irreversible has occurred. As we see in the following passage, Vinca is no longer a child, any more than is Phil.

> "It doesn't? So you'll forgive me for acting like a little girl, so ridiculous?"

She only hesitated a second: "Of course I'm going to forgive you, Phil. But even that won't change a thing."

"About what?"

"About us, Phil."

She spoke with a sibylline softness that he didn't dare challenge further, and in which he didn't dare rejoice. Vinca no doubt followed the steps of his mental twists and turns, since she subtly added: "Do you remember the scenes you made, and the ones I made—it wasn't even three weeks ago—when we were so upset at having to cool off for four or five years before getting married? My poor Phil, I really wish I could turn the clock back and be a child again today."

He waited for her to underline, to comment on that skillful, that insidious "today", hanging in front of him in the pure and blue air of that August night. But Vinca already knew how to arm herself with silence.

He insisted: "So, you're not holding it against me? Tomorrow we'll be . . . we'll be Vinca and Phil, the way we always were? Forever?"

"Forever—if you want it, Phil. . . . C'mon, let's go back inside. Its cold out here."

She hadn't repeated, "the way we always were." But he contented himself with this incomplete vow and with the small, cold hand he held for a moment in his own.

Adolescents arm themselves with silence

"Learning how to arm yourself with silence" is perhaps one of the most telling lines above, in that the choice of whether or not to communicate can feel like one of the new weapons acquired by the adolescent. However, this only feels like a weapon to those who relate to the adolescent, for they must live with the adolescent's right not to communicate as well as the new capacity to think that we discussed in chapter 2. As such, we see a new capacity to relate, which reflects the emergence of a new sense of self. We saw earlier, when we were thinking about the adolescent's peer group, that these aggregates form a foundation upon which the individual adolescent can start to form relationships with those who are different. But this development is paralleled by another going on within them, reflected by the choice whether or not to communicate. Put another way, it could be called the capacity to arm oneself with silence.

The silence of adolescents is perhaps one of the most troubling aspects of the experience of their parents. There can seem to be an insurmountable wall between the two, which can be puzzling and infuriating to both sides as they struggle with their incomprehension. We get a sense of this non-communication when Holden's sister, Phoebe, tells him that "Daddy will kill you". But one way of thinking about this is to imagine that an adolescent is developing a sense of their inner world and seeing it as different from the external circumstances. The cry that "you don't understand me", which can be so infuriating for parents trying desperately to do just that, sometimes stems from the adolescent—having just discovered a new sense of self, which is a struggle to understand—refusing to have it be "understood" by well-meaning parents, because this will subtly threaten to undermine a very private achievement. It is so private that the adolescent is often only barely aware of it, but it makes possible a new kind of detachment that can withstand the pressure of strong feelings that can sweep away the capacity for logical thought that we discussed in chapter 2. As a result, it can often seem very difficult for adults to help, advise, or counsel adolescents, because the mere fact of accepting help seems to threaten adolescents' sense of their maturity. To be helped is for little kids reliant on parents, teachers, or other forms of authority. Help can feel like a usurping of their newly acquired separateness of mind. We can see it in the reaction of Holden suddenly seeming rather tired after hearing the "good advice" of Mr Antolini.

Therefore, when it comes to thinking about maturity, we can see that there will inevitably be at least two views. The adult world will look at the adolescent's behaviour—from the external point of view—and arrive at conclusions that always and quite properly reflect their own perspective, experience, and values. They can do little else—other than abdicate, which they must not do. Adolescents will look at the situation from their own newly won perspective—their own internal view, which will include their own private striving for maturity as they see it themselves and how they think they will be seen by their peers.

What takes priority is not necessarily whatever action is proposed, but the means by which it was conceived as an action—the adolescent's own mind and point of view comes under threat. Nothing brings this into focus like the perennial problem of the time when the adolescent is expected home at night and the fantasies parents will have about what the adolescent is getting up to when away from home, which always lurks in the background of these disagreements. It will come as no reassurance to hard-pressed parents to say that there is no way of avoiding this dilemma. As an adolescent's mind develops and grows towards maturity, such conflicts must occur—and they will come in many guises; but most, if not all, will concern the future. The subject matter of these conflicts usually is about disasters that may potentially befall the adolescent or parents being faced with the disastrous loss of their child. Very often there will be a basis in reality for these fears, and *it helps no parent to suggest that such fears are groundless,* and still less does it help the adolescent.

The point is that these conflicts have to be lived through, and there is no easy formula that says that they can be avoided.

What we can notice is the gradual shift in the adolescent perspective towards parents and the other adults in their lives as they grow older. How and when this happens is unique to each adolescent—it no doubt depends to some degree on the environment in which they grow up, and this environment is inescapably the creation of their parents, be they present or absent.

Maturity and its acquisition is a process that does not finish at mid-adolescence. Yet by the age of 17 the form it will take for each individual adolescent will be well on its way to its final formation. Part of its basis is cognitive development, as we discussed in Chapter 2. But we get a sense of the complexity of this unique experience, which forms each adolescent's quest for maturity, in the first excerpt from the *Le Blé en Herbe* above, when we sense the atmosphere that surrounds Phil's placing his arm into Camille's outstretched hand. The sexual atmosphere created by the mature adult woman in relation to the 16-year-old boy changes the nature of the his action to one that is not a gesture of a child towards its mother but of a man, however immature, towards a woman. But at the same time this narrative is written through Phillipe's eyes and read by us adults—with our adult minds. Hence we can imagine his individual experience and that of adolescents as a whole, extracted through the filter of our own experience as adolescents.

We might take this as just an illustration from a novel, which fortuitously makes a point. The fact that we have noted clear international differences in the nature and intent of sex education suggests the importance of the environment created by parents—in both the material and psychological senses—for the growth to maturity of their adolescent children. Ultimately, maturity reflects a capacity to be objective about the internal and external world. There can be no doubt that each parent provides a model of this capacity for their adolescent children—and from this responsibility there is no escape. Even if the parent concerned is not actually physically present, the effect of the parent's absence will be felt, and there will be a reaction.

A mid-adolescent's response to the absence of a parent

A mid-adolescent came for help expressing a feeling of a lack of confidence and fear when in the presence of other people and a sense that others in his family were false and contemptible. His lack of confidence expressed itself in his feeling that others looked down on him, and in particular he was very anxious about what girls felt about him. He came in his mid-teens at the recommendation of a teacher at the school he was attending. He had been living with his maternal grandmother for the past five years. The significant facts that he reported of his family history were that his mother had suddenly left the family home when he was six; after this, he and his brother had lived with his father for a while. Their father then met and married his stepmother, and they all tried to live together, until the situation broke down and he moved to his maternal grandmother's flat when he was 11. This was experienced as very difficult, and consciously he had little but contempt for his stepfamily, seeing them as superficial and "corny". It was this contempt, of course, that made him prone to seeing the same contempt that he felt others felt for him.

The significance of these facts about his life was not immediately obvious to him because it was the fact of his own experience. The difficulty he had in reflecting upon his experience meant that he expressed his difficulties in the way he behaved in relation to me in the course of his sessions. Thus, for example, at the end of the session he would look at me with an odd combination of fear and hatred and say "see you later" as he left with a slight air of contempt. The combination of these actions, in the one moment, captured beautifully the moment he had in his mind of his mother leaving his father, with whom he identified. He therefore communicated to me the angry, abandoning mother in his mind who, being always present in her absence, left him in a state of fear and helplessness.

The meaning of this moment became increasingly clear to us and paved the way for him to find and visit his mother again for the first time in some years. Up to this point, in his mind his perception of his mother had been that she was harsh and rejecting. He discovered her not to be the violent, heartless bully of his fantasies, but actually someone who was herself depressed. This was a profound shock to him, because it upset all the fantasies he had built up to rationalize what had happened to him. This new mother did not fit the image of the violent mother who had left him and who, he felt, hated him.

He could now see that his fear of what girls thought about him arose from his hatred of women, and in particular his mother. Hence, we could see that this unconscious hatred, which was implied by his conscious fear, had been the stuff out of which the imagined hating mother had been created. His hatred had then to be projected and denied, because acknowledgement of his own hate would mean having to assume responsibility for the departure of his loved object.

The net effect of this psychic manoeuvre had been to void him of his aggression, which led, in turn, to his lack of confidence and the belief that others looked upon him with contempt. However, this lack of confidence was the price exacted for avoiding a sense of his responsibility for his mother's departure—that is, his overriding need to maintain his mother as a good object transformed the hatred of his loved mother into an unconscious belief on his part that his hatred of his mother had driven her away. The consequence of this belief being unconscious was that he was in consciousness afraid of her *as he was of all girls to whom he was attracted.*

We could see how, in the re-encounter with his actual mother, the terrifying imagined mother was thrown into sharp relief and differentiated from his actual mother. This imagined mother had been created in the space left by the departure of his actual mother. It had then powerfully determined his psychic life and the conscious experience of his life. When he could see that this imagined figure, a product of his own mind, had been experienced and perceived as if it were a fact of external reality, there was a considerable reduction in his anxiety after an initial profound shock. There was also a radical shift in his capacity to reflect on his own mind and a realization that he did not necessarily know what was in the mind of the (m)other. The minds of others were there to be discovered and did not need to be automatically thought of as frightening or contemptuous.

Perhaps the confirmation of this hypothesis was the belief that developed in him that he needed to stay in contact with his mother to enable him to have a relationship with a girl. It was this that enabled him to replace the old hating mother with a present alive mother through whom he could create a relationship with a girl. The relationship with his mother went through many ups and downs. In any event, the gradual repair of this relationship did, indeed, enable him to think of having a relationship with a girl, which he successfully achieved.

I think we can see that, in this instance, this mid-adolescent's quest for a sense of maturity and a sense of "feeling real" had been substantially impeded by how he had reacted to his mother's sudden departure and the way he had unwittingly taken responsibility for it. These reactions left him feeling that he could not attain a maturity enabling him to move into adulthood with an abiding sense of his psychological security. He achieved this by going to meet his mother, which took greater courage than one might imagine because he had no idea of the reality that he would find. But he did so; and in so doing he managed a radical reorganization of himself and the relationships he could have with others.

I use the word "organization" here because it captures well a process that may not be obviously apparent. Sometimes, as in the case just described, it requires help from an authoritative adult to achieve. Yet this process of starting to "get organized" is what marks the beginning of the end of mid-adolescence. When this process becomes self-initiated, the adult/parent can start to see the adolescent beginning to achieve the autonomy that is the mark of a genuine maturity. The adolescent seems to know what they want and knows how to achieve it and is becoming aware of their impact on others. When they begin to be aware of what they do not know and know to whom to turn to find out without feeling that their maturity is questioned, then the road to young adulthood is well and truly open.

In chapter 9 we look at this process of starting to get organized from two points of view, the first concerning moving into the world of adult work and finding one's authority through being able to cooperate effectively with others, and the second concerning the organization of sexuality and the finding of a partner. But before considering this, we need to look at a major impediment to this process. One of biggest miseries faced by adolescents is the experience of being bullied. This is by no means unique to adolescence and is to be found in all institutional life at all ages. However, in mid-adolescence the impact of this experience can substantially undermine the individual adolescent's strivings towards maturity.

Note

1. Translated into English as "Green Wheat". The title itself comes from the saying, *"Ne pas manger le blé en herbe"*—in other words, "Don't eat wheat before it is ready" . . . perhaps a plea for a measure of immaturity.

8

on bullying and being bullied

Being bullied is one of the most common causes of human unhappiness and can occur at any time of life. The mid-adolescent is especially prone, because this is a time in life when a mature character is not yet formed. Every day adolescents meet up with their equally immature peers in settings that are intrinsically competitive in terms of pecking orders and territory. If we remember the constant confrontations between the young men of the Montague and Capulet families in fourteenth-century Verona as depicted in *Romeo and Juliet*, we can get a context for the situations in which bullying can occur.

Not for nothing does the Jets' song in *West Side Story* go as follows:

When you're a Jet,
You're a Jet all the way
From your first cigarette
To your last dyin' day.

When you're a Jet,
If the spit hits the fan,
You got brothers around,
You're a family man!

You're never alone,
You're never disconnected!
You're home with your own:
When company's expected,
You're well protected!

Then you are set
With a capital J,
Which you'll never forget
Till they cart you away.
When you're a Jet,
You stay a Jet!

Sondheim's song gives a sense of the importance of the peer group as a group with whom to identify, and how important it is in the inevitable confrontation with other strangers. It may be reassuring to realize that in some way things don't change. Nevertheless, the underlying anxieties bring the same hurt and anguish that they did six hundred years ago.

An advice centre run by bullying.co.uk presents an abundance of correspondence from obviously very distressed adolescents suffering agonies every day as a result of being or feeling different from their peers in some important way. Bullying is the downside of the power of the peer group and is the evidence of the power of the feelings it can generate and harness. This is because a peer group can be very intolerant of differences between its members. We can see in the lyrics of the Jets' song the value placed on uniformity and conformity. It seems to suggest that if we are all the same, then there will be no differences between us. The problem with difference is that if you are different, then you might turn out inferior to someone. Bullying is all about making someone feel inferior, with the implication that the bully feels superior.

The agony of being a victim

This letter is a composite of many such letters received by an advice centre for adolescents.

> Dear ____
>
> Can you tell me how I can move to a new school? I'm 14 and I can't face school any more. My grades at school have gone right down and I'm bunking off when my mum's at work because I can't face all the lessons I have with the bullies. I get called names about my weight and I have nobody to go around with at break. When I sit down with my packed lunch the others get up and move away. I'm taking so much time off that my mum is going to find out soon. I've told my head of year and she spoke to them but they're still doing it. This is making me feel very depressed and I've self-harmed a few times.

Reading such a letter gives an immediate sense of isolation and hopelessness in the victims of bullying. It shows that victims of bullying can feel caught between the need to be breaking away from the family and the need for protection from the world by their family. Children who are depressed, for whatever reason, may be targets of bullying because they are unable to join in the manic exuberance of the peer group and as a result feel that they are seen as "sad" by their peers, leaving them feeling that they don't have any friends and will never make any. This, in turn, can lead to school avoidance, with all its consequences for educational attainment. This can also be hidden from the parents by the bullied child because to talk about it can feel very humiliating.

The despair expressed by this young person is as heartbreaking as is the terrible waste suffered by society as a result. The spare fragments of experience are indicators of a widespread phenomenon that is hard to understand partly because it is so widespread. Very few escape the experience of being bullied, which is no doubt part of the reason for it being apparently endemic and intractable.

Reading this letter naturally brings sympathy for the victim of some bully or bullies for whom any understanding beyond condemnation might seem odd. But we can get further in our understanding of bullying if we think about the social milieu in which bullying occurs. Searching for cause and effect requires looking at the personality and history of both victim and bully, their respective family histories, and the social and community setting. Studying the personality characteristics of victims and bullies confirms what might be expected, with the victim being cautious, sensitive, and quiet and the bully apparently gaining in both self-esteem and prestige from their success in dominating and inflicting personal and psychological injury on others. However, one interesting finding showed that the level of bullying reported by children attending remedial classes or full-time special classes was twice that for non-remedial children (O'Moore & Hillery, 1989).

Understanding the bully

There is clear evidence that bullying can be seen as a component of a more generalized antisocial and conduct-disordered behaviour pattern. Indeed, it has been suggested on the basis of research evidence that bullying behaviour in school is strongly influenced by parenting and family environment and may flow through generations in a cycle of violence. In general, parents whose children become involved in bullying, regardless of role, are more likely to have problems of poor family functioning and an insecure attachment relationship with their child and to be perceived negatively by their child (Smith & Myron-Wilson, 1998). Parents of bullies are said to be more likely to use a harsh discipline style, and the whole family may be distant or "disengaged" with each other. Parents, especially mothers, of victims, on the other hand, are said to overprotective, and the family as a whole can be seen as overly close or "enmeshed".

Helpful though these views are, looking further at the social context suggests that some institutions can create a climate within which a sense of inadequacy becomes a currency in how different members of a social group or organization assign status to one another. This status differential will be immediately recognizable to those within the group but may be scarcely visible to those outside it. If we stop to look at it for long enough, we will, of course, recognize this from our own experience.

However, it is horribly true that victims of bullying can live in very private hell, partly because it is humiliating to admit to injury to one's self-esteem. Indeed, to have to admit to it can almost seem to add to it. It is not uncommon for victims to blame themselves, leading them to self-harm and, in some cases, make suicide attempts, which are sometimes tragically successful. Why should such an apparently irrational response occur to this kind of assault? One cannot easily generalize, but it may be that in some circumstances victims believe that they are somehow responsible for their situation, perhaps because they see that some seem to be able to avoid it and others perpetrate it. In hating their helplessness, they can blame themselves without realizing they are doing so.

It will be clear that bullying has a serious effect on all those who suffer it. When it is serious enough to reach the notice of the psychiatric services, it tends to be both obvious and chronic in nature. This is at the extreme end of a long continuum that probably occurs to some degree in any situation where there is a degree of competition, with the implication that "losers" are somehow inferior to those who prevail. As we saw in the example of children in remedial education, where individuals find themselves in a group where *all* are implicitly identified as inferior to those not in such a group, bullying seems to occur to a greater extent than would be expected. The implication of this finding is that bullying cannot be understood fully by considering the victim and the bully in isolation. Institutions may unwittingly create the conditions conducive to bullying because individuals in it struggle to disavow the feelings of inferiority implied by being a member of that institution at all.

How parents can help

From the parents' point of view, the main difficulty in helping a child who is being bullied to the point where it is disabling is to realize how unhappy they are. Being bullied can be so humiliating that that victims keep it to themselves as far as possible. Although this may seem in itself to imply a criticism of the parent, we have already seen how private mid-adolescents can become. Finding the right path between interested but over-intrusive concern and benign indifference can be one of the real difficulties of parenthood at this stage in their adolescent's development.

The bullying.co.uk website gives very helpful advice to parents who suspect that their children are being bullied. Briefly, they suggest that parents should be aware of certain signs that something may be amiss. Some of these are obvious: coming home with torn clothes or with cuts and bruises, possibly suggesting that the child has been in a fight or has been roughly pushed around, or noticing that something valued by the child has "gone missing" inexplicably, or that dinner money has been "lost".

Other signs may be less obvious. Bullied children may suddenly seem depressed and reluctant to go out or to go to school. They may be bad-tempered without an obvious reason or withdrawn as if there is something of which they are ashamed. They may seem isolated from old familiar friends or have fallen out with them. They may seem to be aggressive towards younger and more defenceless brothers or sisters or to others outside the family.

If you find out that your child is being bullied, this can be very distressing, and you may feel that something must be done about it immediately. Bullying Online suggests, however, that the worst thing you can do is go storming into somewhere that looks responsible—like a school—demanding action. In the end, a calmer more considered approach gets better results.

What it can mean for parents when their child is being bullied

In extreme cases, which reach the notice of the psychiatric services, the disturbance experienced by either the victim or the bully is usually clear.

For example, a 15-year-old boy who had been diagnosed with Attention Deficit Hyperactivity Disorder and was continuously bullying other children said that from an early age at school he was always seen as trouble and he saw himself as the school scapegoat. He had been moved from mainstream school to an EBD (emotional and behavioural disorder) school. He had not liked moving to the EBD school at first but said that he would not consider returning to mainstream now. His father was reported as having used excessive physical punishment to try to control the boy's overactive and aggressive behaviour. The boy believed that this gave him an attitude, and he started to bully other children, call them names, and to get into fights. These behaviours made him feel better, and he was able to secure money for cigarettes and sometimes alcohol. He thought it unlikely that anyone would come to any great harm as a result of his bullying, but he had not really given it much thought. He said he hated his father and most adults, although one teacher at school was "OK". He did not know what he would do when he left school.

Examples like this suggest that for parents the most painful aspect of finding that their child is either being a bully or being bullied is the self-examination that may be needed to reach an understanding of what is going on. The boy in the example apparently thought that it was his father's attempts to discipline him that gave him an attitude, leading him to bully others. Why his father did this we cannot tell, any more than the boy probably could. It would have been the only world that he knew, and he was not yet in a position to know about other possible ways of being fathered. Insofar as his father provided a model for him to relate to others, it may well have been inevitable that he would attack others in whom he identified the same kind of inferiority as he believed his father saw in him. This leads to an insight into how relations between parents and their adolescent children can get very tangled.

Bullying.online's warning to parents to avoid storming into a school demanding action is ample evidence that it is all too easy to leap to the defence of one's child and search for a scapegoat before realizing that you see yourself in your adolescent—no matter how non-compliant they may seem. In being sympathetic with one's bullied teenager, it is likely that one is implicitly remembering one's own experiences of being bullied. In leaping to your child's defence, you are perhaps doing what you hoped then would be done for you—or, indeed, possibly what was done for you. Even if you feel unsympathetic, feeling that this is the world of hard knocks and that teenagers had better learn to defend themselves, you inevitably create a model for your adolescent to adopt . . . or reject.

The implication is that parents inevitably see themselves in their adolescent children as they develop towards adulthood. They will sometimes see the parts of themselves of which they are proud and at other times aspects of which they are ashamed. It is probably also true that your adolescent children will identify with you far more than they would like to think

. . . or indeed realize. In truth, they have little option but to do this, and it seems to make little difference to the situation, even if the actual parent is absent. An absent parent will be recreated in the adolescent's imagination and possibly have even greater influence because of their absence than they would have if they were present.

This gap in the awareness of the similarities between parents and their adolescent children causes as much difficulty, if not more, as the apparent differences in attitude and belief. For parents to realize that when they look at what is apparently unacceptable behaviour in their adolescent children they can be looking at what they find unacceptable in themselves takes some strength and maturity. Yet it seems that this maturity is what is required by adolescents who look to their parents when they struggle to find their own sense of themselves and their own authority.

9

starting to get organized: leaving mid-adolescence to enter the world of others

"I must create a system or be enslav'd by some other man's"
from "Jerusalem" by William Blake.

As mid-adolescence draws to a close, we begin to see an increasing sense of integration as the adolescent starts to relate to us in a more organized way. The task for an adolescent is to find a way of engaging with and being effective in the adult world. This entails finding ways of being with others in such a way that both achieve fruitful ends. This encounter with the world of others enables a process of internal organization through which ambitions and desires can be realized, given the limits imposed by reality. In doing this, the adolescent's developing internal organization permits the emergence of a *sense of identity: the adolescent's sense of who they are.*

When this is happening, you may find that they start to talk to you in a new way. An impulsiveness of thought and a sense of compliance with you, or reaction against you, will seem to have given way to something more balanced, allowing their own mind and your mind to exist together effectively and happily. No longer is there an implicit but constant struggle. Something seems to have become more organized, and a new kind of cooperation seems possible.

In this chapter we look at this process of becoming organized in two ways. First we consider how the mid-adolescent begins to engage with the adult world through work and taking responsibility for some task outside the confines of home and family—in other words, work for and with other people. These days, a majority continue education beyond the statutory school-leaving age, and some continue on into their early twenties. We will not be thinking of work in this educational sense, even though this education process will progressively be in the context of career aspirations.

We then look at this process by considering the experience of finding a partner and of falling in love. In previous chapters we have thought about this finding of another person in a number of ways: adolescents' sexual activity, how they relate to others in their peer groups, and the development of new cognitive abilities. All this may be brought together in the emergence of a relationship that seems longer-lasting than the fleeting crushes of early adolescence.

For parents, new prospects will begin to open up. The child who seemed such a permanent fixture in their lives is now on the verge of moving out into the world. If they develop a relationship, then someone new is brought into the home. The arrival of this person will have a different significance from the comings and goings of friends from the neighbourhood.

Entering the world of work

Testing themselves in the adult world takes place through the effective contributions adolescents make to others. They can do this in a variety of situations: in friendships, love, hobbies, sport, home, local activities and movements, and in money-earning work. Money represents in real terms—not just symbolically, like pocket money—a means of exchange. The fact of an adult body and greater autonomy means that the adolescent is now capable of driving a car and pursuing dangerous—in the sense of life-threatening—sports and activities. Thus, the adolescent is now a temporal being, which means facing limits—among them, death—in a new way. Thus the adolescent can begin to relate to others and also can place himself in time in a different way. He now has a past and a potential future.

Struggles for autonomy will probably have been encountered by now in such matters as when the adolescent is expected home at night, pocket money, and which friends are approved of by the parents as suitable company and which are not. Adolescents and their parents growing up in a community where all know each other are at a considerable advantage, because it is much easier to establish a consensus about the question of what is appropriate and/or "fair". In larger and more diffuse urban communities adolescents' protests to their parents that "you don't understand" about these matters may well, alas, have a truth to them. Questions of how the adolescent gets about and with whom all relate to the adolescent discovering a "social life". But as adolescents get older, they gain more autonomy. Society, in the guise of the law, recognizes this, as discussed earlier.

Going through this period will always involve an element of risk and a consequent feeling of danger. Adolescents will begin to feel more "grown-up" as they spread their wings. Each time it happens, parents will hold their breath, even if only slightly. More worrying, perhaps, is the adolescent who apparently refuses to budge from home: it can seem that they are refusing for some reason the inevitability of adulthood. Parents may begin to fear their children will never fly the nest and remain like guests who have outstayed their welcome. There is great variation in the process of leaving home, brought about in part by the expectations of cultural norms. But this variation notwithstanding, the ambivalence felt by adolescents towards the inevitability of the loss of childhood is probably universal, given the nature of the attachment to parents from birth onwards.

As mentioned above, another way in which adolescents enter the adult world is by beginning to work for money. This gives both a sense of autonomy and choice. *Work* is often equated with *money-earning activity*. *Self-earned money* has the great advantage of conferring the *freedom to choose* the means of one's satisfactions and to stand apart in independence from the family in deciding how some of one's desires are to be met. However, earning money in itself is a narrow definition of work because it relates to some of the ends achieved by the individual. If we broaden the definition in terms of *intentionally making effective contributions* to others, then conscientious unpaid service to family, friends, or the public would be considered work. This accords well enough with general usage. A consequence of making effective an contribution to others is learning about *being responsible* in terms of being answerable for one's actions.

What differentiates work from *play* is that one works for something more than immediate personal pleasure. Conscientious *discipline* is intrinsic to any work. It seems that work must be rewarded, not necessarily in money, and it is hard to conceive of a person going on disciplining himself for no recompense at all. Reward can often be from the knowledge of being useful, people's gratitude, pride of achievement, a little relief from fear of a tyrant, or even neurotic pleasure in suffering. *To work, therefore, is to be part of a social system engaging with external reality. To play is to practice the intertwining of one's external and internal reality.*

When leaving school at 16, young people are faced with a variety of situations: friendships, hobbies, sport, home, loves, and, in some cases, paid work itself. They have to assess intuitively their contributions to and satisfactions from all these in shaping the style of their life and finding a satisfactory sense of themselves. This is done only half-consciously, probably in a blundering fashion, and is naturally often seriously avoided. But making an assessment of our contributions is of central importance in growing up; it takes *courage* to step outside one's delusions to see one's efforts as others see them. If this process misfires, a person is left flitting about in self-deception, with a very shaky sense of self-esteem and integrity. Furthermore, these contributions involve effects on others, so the scrutiny of *conscience* plays a central part in this process of finding self-satisfaction. It also means facing and recognizing the effects of others.

As adolescents reach out into the adult world, they will find tasks of varying degrees of *repetition,* together with the opportunity for *creativity* and *responsibility*. Let us consider some of the personal strains and satisfactions involved in these. As adults, our ideas about repetitive work might be shaped by memories of the rust-belt industries of the not-so-distant past. However, the periodicity of the body means that any work involving the care of living beings, be they human or animal, imposes a repetitive routine that must be related to in a responsible way. This seems to constitute the drudgery of repetitive work more than gross physical toil. Learning to accept and bear drudgery is an essential means of learning about the difficulties and distastes arising from the responsibility entailed in adult work.

Both repetition and creativity were exercised in school, so they will not be new to the adolescent. But full responsibility for a task upon which other people depend will be relatively new. Responsibility for a task means being entrusted with its successful completion. The experience of being trusted in this way contributes to the individual finding their authority.

John Bazalgette (1978) studied adolescents' experience of their transition from school to work and in particular the role that adults play in offering a model on the basis of which adolescents can begin to discover their own authority. In the following quotation from this study, he describes the way the young people could, in starting to see the functioning of a factory and the components it produced, develop from this a view of their own role in relation to others and how they complement others to form a whole within which they can see themselves.

> The patterns of work in all the firms studied involved young employees in collaborative relationships with colleagues and supervisors. That is to say, in work, a person joined a team, which was usually striving to achieve something. The young person's part might be small in itself, but the goal for the team called for something from everyone. In the school "work" was an individual activity and one's success was assumed to be principally a function of one's own effort, though some feeling of teacher's efforts having some influence on the pupils was common and understandable. There was also a feeling that the product of working in employment was tangible: one could see a stud completed, recognise an assembled relay, appreciate a completed sale. More than this it did not take a great feat of imagination to envisage how some of the parts fitted together to make an intelligible whole: as the operator said at Reliable Engineering "if it were not for what we make, cars would fall to bits on the road".

These processes of learning a function in an organization are ordinary and natural and require no direct intervention to make them happen. But if they are to happen, the adolescent needs some access to an adult world of work. This description of the growth of responsibility will probably take away some of its possibly pedantic and dull connotations. Its essence does carry a necessary solemnity. It entails conserving and is thus, as it were, conservative. And in many ways it is antithetical to romantic exploration and personal creativity. It is perhaps the loss of romantic freedom that makes responsibility loathsome to many people, young and old. They seem to associate it with dullness and hence deadness. Perhaps they are frightened, too, not only of depression, but also of possible guilt. Balanced off against this is the sense of being part of an essential whole in the external world ("if it weren't for us, the cars would fall to bits"), and this perception of being in a structure reflects a capacity for internal structuring that is taking place in the young person's mind. Hence we see something getting organized internally and externally at the same time.

For the mid-adolescent, the question of what career to pursue is likely to be based as much on image as upon any real understanding of what is involved in the doing of it. Many will reply, when asked what they want to do, that they don't know, which is in many cases both reasonable and the truth. By "image", I mean that they imagine a person doing something and want to be that person. This occurs much earlier, with young children saying they want to be a footballer or a rock star or, in earlier days, a train driver. But the prospect of adulthood is beginning to gather in the adolescents' minds because the education system begins to force itself upon them by requiring choices to be made. "Work experience" at school is an effort to make this mysterious world of work a little more realistic for adolescents, and together with the experience of doing something with adults comes the experience of autonomy, responsibility, and self-discipline.

This will have begun in school, because no matter the subject, course work and its attendant deadlines give an experience of responsibility and self-discipline. The new element of work is that an adult wants something from the adolescent, and there is an immediate sanction if the adult's need is not satisfied. The adult supervisor can point to the door with immediate effect much sooner than can a parent or the school. One very intelligent adolescent went through what was, for her, the mortifying experience of being sacked from a job as a bar-girl after being warned that she was chattering too much with her workmates. She was both furious and ashamed, but it was a salutary introduction to the world of adult discipline in the workplace.

Much work requires a large amount of choice, and therefore the opportunities for this experience of an internal organization with others can take many forms in many different contexts. Thus a skilled fitter will have more choice as to how to go about a task than does a data entry operator. The greater the freedom of invention, the more *skilled* does the individual have to be. This entails self-disciplined sacrifice of idiosyncratic whims. For, like a mother with a newborn child, the worker has to submit to the limits of the tools and the material. But after perhaps years of self-discipline, he, his body, and his materials have formed a sort of unity. Here we see a strange outcome of self-discipline: this is a controlled loss of the boundary of the self, so that self, tools, and materials become almost the same.

Art requires skill and more besides: it starts with a person becoming "at one" with or the same as his or her object and materials. To be good, he must lose himself in them. This recalls the loosening of the boundaries of the self, referred to frequently in previous chapters. And then, as also mentioned, the creative artist tries to allow a personal abstract vision to arise, which he reproduces. It is usually only after years of devoted practice, when he is master of himself and at one with his materials, that this is possible. A skilled worker knows truthfully about his materials and their functions. A botcher makes much *pretence* of knowledge, and deceit can then, of course, be towards himself as much as to any customer. A true artist seems to have a particular form of deep conscience, which works in a way that is baffling to many people. He feels a fundamental responsibility to his art, to purify his abstract vision and communicate it to others. He is often not so deeply concerned about the everyday effect on other people and can even be indolent and thoughtless about common sociability.

The purpose of making this rather obvious distinction between the skilled worker and the botcher is to emphasize the difference between the individual who accepts the limitations of his materials and ultimately himself and someone who is contents with remaining in an illusion of his capabilities. The shock suffered by the chattering bar-girl was because she had not quite grasped that the landlord was concerned with serving customers, and that was the priority. In the new world of work, the other is a stranger to whom a responsibility is owed. These strangers are called supervisors and customers in the adult world.

The emergence of an identity

We have just been considering the emerging late-adolescent facing the situations of paid work, friends, family, and leisure. Here, each specific activity can be considered as offering a *role.* At any one time, a person has a multiplicity of these. When, and if, he has found a *personal patterning of these roles,* and where the emotionally charged contradictions between them have been more or less disentangled, and which then *together give him inner satisfactions, he then usually experiences a sense of meaningful wholeness and well-being. He is then on the way to an adult identity and starting to get organized.*

Eric Erikson's (1950) idea of *identity* has now become part of our everyday language. Thus we hear of "work identity", "sexual identity", "class identity", "racial identity", "national identity". Because these concepts have entered into everyday thought and parlance so quickly and powerfully, they must have a deep relevance. In drawing attention to them here, we must realize that they are slightly different from the overall individual self-identity we have just introduced. Sexual, racial, national, class, and work identities refer to the individual's feeling of belonging to certain groups as distinct from others.

A person must experience a multiplicity of such identities, because everyone belongs to several of these groups at once. They are, as it were, sub-identities of a person's overall feeling of being himself, his self-identity. Self-identity is something that develops from inside and is the consequence of the growing maturity that we discussed earlier.

This identity, though delimited by forces of one's culture as well as inheritance, is essentially idiosyncratic and private to each individual. We have been slowly leading up to this concept of identity, particularly when we have been stressing that an honest scrutiny of our conscience is essential in finding *integration*. For it is by self-scrutiny that we assess and balance the enjoyments of our own life with those of others. In chapter 2 we discussed the emergence of abilities that make this self-scrutiny possible.

Residues of childhood

Even though the mid-adolescent begins to assume the responsibilities of being an adult and dependent childhood attitudes slip into the background, this does not mean that they have died within them. The childish parts will—indeed, to some extent must—remain active, often unconsciously. If they are not assimilated into life, their insistent repetition may prove disturbing in one way or another. We cannot discuss this fully here, but a little introspection will probably make it plain to the reader that one experiences urges that continue more or less unchanged from our childhood.

Here are a couple of illustrations (Rainer et al., 2005).

A young boy was brought up in the country. His father ran a progressive boarding-school, which was regarded with some suspicion by the local people. The boy's mother cared little about this and ran her family with a back-to-nature philosophy. Her pigs, goats, hand-loom weaving, and homemade pots were unusual and were laughed about in the neighbourhood. The young boy grew up isolated from the local children, though he went to school with them. He was baffled by them and envied their conventional toys and games, so that he rarely felt at ease to join them. When he grew up, he became a schoolmaster, like his parents. His resemblance to them seemed to end there, however, for he went to work in a city and was more conventional in his ways. He was respected and very well liked, so that he quickly became head of a department. However, as soon as he cast off his professional mantle, he was crippled with shyness. He could not bring himself to be at all intimate with others in the neighbourhood. When not at work, people outside his family seemed like a race apart. They were experienced as looking askance at him, just as they had done years earlier.

We can see in this example how childhood and early adolescent relationships with peers were repeated as this man sought to find a way of both identifying and dis-identifying with his parents. It seems that the lack of childhood contact with peers interfered with his capacity to find his identity beyond the parental model in the occupational sense and profoundly affected his ability to form social relationships in his adult life.

In the next example, we can only, in truth, speculate on the forces that propelled this boy out of his home at a comparatively young age and why the prospect of failure brought him close to suicide. However, this example illustrates how an individual's history might be incorporated into a developing idea of an occupational role, which gives powerful expression to his idea of himself as an adult.

Another boy, many years ago, was among the oldest in a family of many children. He was very fond of his mother, but each year brought another birth, so that he had but little of her company. He took this stoically, and in fact became particularly admired by his family for his bravery, both at home and in childhood exploits. His mother died when he was 10, and his father struggled on alone to bring up the family. Two years later the young boy said he wanted to relieve his father of one mouth to feed; he was determined to join the Navy. His father gratefully accepted this further demonstration of bravery.

When he was 18, after six years at sea, the young man fell ill and was invalided home from the East. On the ship on the way back he seems to have gone through an acute adolescent crisis. He became aware that he had no future in the Navy and could see no way of life that would fulfil him. He wondered whether to throw himself overboard and finish it all. Then a "radiant orb was suspended in his mind's eye". He exclaimed, "I will be a hero and, confiding in Providence, will brave every danger".

Later in adult life this is just what he did. Lord Nelson became a brave hero not only to his family, but to England at large and to succeeding generations of schoolboys.

In both these examples we can see elements of adult identity. Simultaneously creative and neurotic, these are, nevertheless, organized into a subjective identity. Perhaps Nelson, in leaving home to go to sea, was unconsciously searching for his dead mother as well as making room for others at home. When illness catastrophically threatened to sever him from the Navy, suicide seemed to be an option. But then the idea of "confiding in Providence" was, perhaps, a new avenue to his mother, which incorporated the fact of his mother's death. Later on, Nelson's heroism seems to have been close to a suicidal tendency. We might say that Providence, or Kismet, had its final word at the Battle of Trafalgar because of Nelson's insistence on effectively offering himself as a target to the French snipers. However, we might speculate that Nelson had found a way of incorporating his devotion for his beloved mother and compensating for his resentment of his siblings in the manner of his life and the conduct leading to his death.

Compromise and adult identity

This need to incorporate childhood needs and integrate them with the demands of the adult world means that the adolescent has to learn the skills of compromise. Compromise is not an activity confined to relationships with others. Sometimes this is very difficult and is reacted to by becoming very idealistic in the political or social sense. There may be violent arguments with parents about these issues, which can take a political form or arguments over what is "just". In a sense this will involve a kind of playful "button-pushing" by adolescents as they test their parents' actual beliefs but also express all kinds of feelings and fears about the adult world. In most cases they should probably be taken very seriously and not written off as a part of "the phase they are going through". At some level, they are inevitably just that, but such anxieties cannot be dismissed, because that gives adolescents the feeling that they are being treated like children.

We can now see a wider significance of D. H. Lawrence's thought that adolescence was the "hour of the stranger". In one sense, the "stranger" represents the prospect of what adolescents feel they will become with the arrival of the new instinctual urges experienced from puberty. With this sense of what one might possibly become comes a new sense of how others seem. An obvious example is the new experience of the opposite sex, and the desire that they provoke means that the individual feels different, and so does the object of his desire. "Strangers", beyond the confines of the family and immediate neighbourhood of childhood, come to the adolescent in a variety of forms. Basically, however, they either represent something inescapable about the external world—as in the case of "customers"—or they bring about the possibility of actualizing ambitions and fantasies stemming from their inner feelings—as in the case of sexual partners.

All adolescents exist in a generational framework. No matter how disrupted their lives may have been, the biological "facts of life" or how they came into being have an inescapable effect on how adolescents understand their history and expect their futures to unfold. With puberty, the actuality of their sexual body, with its power to reproduce, introduces the fact of a "stranger" without whom that reproduction cannot occur. We have to add that the experience of orgasm in a sexually mature body creates quite a new dimension to the expectation and experience of pleasure, because it offers the experience of the dissolution of the boundaries between the self and the other. When this is coupled to all the cognitive and intellectual developments that will by now have occurred, we can see that pleasure *given and taken with another* can potentially be experienced, even if not all achieve that experience.

For some, this experience is very threatening because of the dependence that is implied by these new kinds of relationship. This dependence can imply a loss of control and the threat of helplessness. The implicit threat of such an experience, arising from the prospect of the temporary loss of control and autonomy, may sometimes be short-circuited through a heavy use of drugs—if these are available.

In the example of the schoolteacher discussed earlier, we could see how the ambitions and expectations of parents form something with which the adolescent will identify, wittingly or not, or else react against by being determined to be as unlike the parents as possible. In the example above this relates to the world of others in the social and occupational sense. We now have to think about the ways in which the parental relationships affect the adolescent and shape the ways in which their relationships develop and unfold. We have seen earlier how powerfully adolescents will identify with their parents, even if they consciously wish to be as different from them as possible. Nowhere is this more pronounced than in the adolescent's experience of the parents' relationship. Puberty adds a genital sexual dimension, with a powerful influence on the adolescent's experience of sexual relationships. Equally, the parents' conception of their own sexual experience will inevitably influence how they perceive their adolescent's relationships, especially their sexual dimension.

The position of parents

In the account above of the encounter of the mid-adolescent with the adult world, we can see that it provides many opportunities for adolescents, which they may either seize or avoid. It is inevitable that there will be reactions by parents to what they see of their adolescent's reactions. It is equally inevitable that adolescents will be very sensitive to what they see of their parents' reaction. This is the arena in which the question of giving the time to be immature may be very necessary, and there are no rules to guide us in the individual case. And yet all parents have before them is the individual who is their adolescent child. The "gap year", which has become something of an institution for middle-class adolescents forging their way up the education ladder, seems to be a response to the dangers of foreclosing on the opportunity to explore the world so that adolescents can "find themselves".

The mid-adolescent looking forward to leaving school and entering work or further education will, of course, be largely concerned with anticipating these changes in life. It is a bit like the anticipation of puberty and arouses the same mixed feelings of thrill and dread. Teenage depression, dread, and withdrawal has the potential to create tremendous conflicts between parental ambitions and/or forebodings. There will be times when, to the average parent, realism in the adolescent seems in short supply.

The problem is that parents—contrary to the belief of their adolescent child that "they do not understand"—believe they understand only too well what is happening but, in their perception of their adolescent, see the situation through the lens of their own history and anxieties. As their adolescent negotiates this transition into the adult world, it will be a time of difficulty and distaste for parents that doesn't confine itself to education and work. This period is often the time of the first serious relationship. Gone are the fleeting flirtations and temporary broken hearts of early adolescence. Parents have to start getting used to the prospect of new members of the family, and all their own experience will inform them again, with uncertain effectiveness.

Falling in love

The first directly sexual features of an adolescent's turning away from infantile emotional ties to their parents are often crushes on other people. These can have a disconnected and primitive all-or-nothing quality about them because they can seem to parents to be based on a feature of the desired person. It is not that their child seems to want their object of desire but wants to be like them. When taken into the sexual arena, it is the difference between having sex and making love. It is a bit like wanting to be rock star because it would be wicked to be one. It is based on the image of the other rather than on the experience of being one, with all the responsibilities, difficulties, and distastes that that entails.

Here are two examples of girls reflecting on their boyfriends:

> I am in love with Joel more than anyone, it is I think because he, like me, is half in love with death. (A 15-year-old.)
>
> I only fall for hard men. I think it is because they are the only ones who could stand my violent temper. (A 17-year-old.)

Why are these abstracted parts of a person's character fallen for with such deep personal meaningfulness? The girl who gave the second example gives a clue. She seems to sense that she needs someone to control the rages she cannot manage herself. She is, then, looking for someone to complement her, whereas the girl who is "half in love with death" seeks to identify with someone like herself. It seems that who is chosen reflects something that the adolescent sees in themselves even if this realization is barely conscious.

In the case of a crush, at least one aspect of this kind of falling in love involves finding a characteristic in which we feel deficient. We would expect that a person would feel extremely humble compared to their adored one. This is certainly the case with a crush. Idealization is a facet of love. However, the trouble is that this sort of loving courts disaster because the lover loves an ideal rather than someone real. We can expect even slight misunderstandings to lead our devoted lover to switch to violent hatred at being betrayed. This is certainly likely to happen with immature crushes. What is more, they are *unstable,* since idealization of the loved one tends to *deplete* self-esteem; a lover readily becomes explosively envious. Only when the *idealization is reciprocated* does this self-depletion receive a counterbalance of idealization of the self.

Obviously this is not a complete unravelling or understanding of the crush. The girl quoted above who was in love with Joel says, for instance, that she loves him because he is, *like herself,* "half in love with death". Some adults might say that she has found a comrade in her suffering: the two lovers—alienated from the rest of humanity, as they see it—can understand and comfort each other like babes in the wood. The lovers themselves might see it quite differently, because they would see it as having found someone who understands them. This understanding may stand in opposition to the adolescent's experience of their parents who may be experienced—almost by definition—as being incapable of understanding. If so, one sees here Joel becoming a Romeo inevitably made to be in conflict with Juliet's paternal figure.

We see here two ways in which a sense of complementarity begins to be experienced. By finding one's "other half", one finds something that one feels is missing in oneself. On the other hand, by finding a kindred spirit, the misery resulting from the loneliness of difference is somehow assuaged. Neither incorporates the complementarities of the sexual body or the need for the couple to relate to the external world. And need it necessarily do so? At this stage, the mid-adolescent needs to experience intimate relationships beyond the family in all their joy and potential heartache. When parents see their adolescent with an "unsuitable" girlfriend or boyfriend, we can be sure that the adolescent is working something out in relation to the parents.

We could see in *Romeo and Juliet* that these issues can create very powerful tensions and feelings between parents and their adolescent children. It is also a time of great happiness when all goes well. But to bring a taste of these powerful feelings, let's look at a particular instance of an adolescent's sexual development that has the potential to arouse a great deal of anxiety: whether the adolescent is choosing a partner who is homosexual or one who is heterosexual. In modern parlance, the anxiety concerns whether the adolescent will be straight or gay/lesbian. Put another way, what kind of "stranger" will become their child's complementary other?

Falling in love: the stranger becomes an other

When mid-adolescents venture into the world of others (or strangers), most will come into situations where they feel a sexual desire and attraction for someone who is initially a stranger. What I mean by "the stranger becoming an other" is a process in which someone who is initially unknown to the adolescent is attracted to and by them, and a process of getting to know them then starts. The question is whether this stranger will become a significant other in the adolescent's life—not just another person, but someone significant in whom there is a personal investment and a hope that a deep personal satisfaction will emerge in both of them as a result of their relationship. But this is grown-up language. When the adolescent first has this experience, it will be a strange one. It will inevitably bring the idea of no longer being a child and eventually leaving home.

Parents will be aware of this aspect of their child's life and will have emotional reactions to it. These will range from apprehension to joy, with what will be a curiosity about who it is that their child is bringing home. Who appears will be as much a stranger to the parents as initially to their child. It will seem like a statement and be an event about which it is impossible to be neutral and detached. The point is that this stranger may become part of the adolescent's life and thus part of the parents' life. Or not—at the outset it is impossible to know.

To bring out some of the potential feelings, let us think about the question of whether who is brought home is someone of the same gender as the child or of the opposite one. One of the few indisputable facts about sexual development is that some people develop a *sexual orientation* such that they are drawn to the opposite gender, and others are drawn to the same one. Some, therefore, have a heterosexual orientation and others a homosexual one. The determinants of this phenomenon have not been clearly understood, but it does seem that this is established by early adulthood, after which it does not often change. Although this aspect of sexuality is often thought about in a moralizing way, it seems to be both inevitable and universal: it will occur regardless of cultural norm. Culture will affect how it is viewed by members of the culture, but it will not affect its occurrence, even if the cultural norms seem to drive it into "the closet".

Whatever culture dictates, the point I seek to make here is to give you the opportunity to think about what you might feel about the kind of "stranger" your adolescent brings home through this device of asking you to think about a situation in which someone who seems irreconcilably different from your own values and outlook turns up. This applies both to those readers who are parents and those who are adolescents. Here is a situation in which it is difficult to envisage right and wrong answers—but the feelings stirred in these situations can be so strong as to lead to murder being committed.

This fact of human sexuality is set against the fact that physiology dictates that we are all brought into the world as a result of the meeting of a spermatozoidan and an ovum. Somewhere and sometime a man and a woman were involved—even if they never met as people, as is the case when a woman is impregnated with sperm given by a donor. All parents have therefore inevitably been, in this sense, heterosexual in bringing their child into the world, even if they are or become homosexual in the way that they live. This means that the recognition of their child's homosexuality involves accepting a difference. Some find this very hard, and the phrase "coming out" clearly means that anguish and conflict is expected. The fact that, for many years, homosexuality was a criminal offence in this country and is still viewed with disgust in many parts of the world today gives ample evidence of the anxieties that this aspect of sexual development engenders.

The great majority of mid-adolescents will not have adopted such an irrevocable position. This is true even though some may think that they have. By definition, it is therefore a part of sexual development at this stage. Sometimes it is thought of as having involved some kind of choice, but in most cases no conscious choice is involved at all. It just seems to happen—perhaps the best evidence we have that much goes into the development of our sexuality that is outside our consciousness or deliberate intention. To complicate the situation, some people seem to develop as bisexual—that is, they profess to be sexually attracted to either sex. We have already discussed how one adolescent can be attracted to another by seeing something in that other that seems missing in themselves. They can also see something that they seem to have in common with them. Hence there is much in falling in love that involves recognizing something in the desired other that the recognizer feels they need.

A great deal of thought has gone into trying to understand why sexual orientation can take different forms. The range of different ideas makes it difficult readily to understand one individual. Parents trying to understand their own children are confronted not only with trying to understand them but also with trying to understand their own emotional reactions. Not least of the difficulties is that of inevitably, in some sense, heterosexual parents trying to understand empathically how a homosexual person can find someone of their own gender erotically attractive when they are only used to seeing someone of the opposite sex attractive in this way. An intriguing aspect is that somehow attraction and revulsion seem to need to be in balance, such that if one orientation becomes attractive, the alternative prospect can be experienced as repulsive.

Finding someone with whom to have a relationship involves a process of finding someone with whom the adolescent can somehow feel and be themselves. It is similar in some ways to the search for an occupation that enables them to be themselves. This process is not complete as the mid-adolescent moves into late adolescence, but it may well have started. Being able to start to become organized is the result of the beginnings of the development of maturity. The mid-adolescent, taking the momentous step from pubertal crush to an actual approach to a potential boy- or girlfriend, opens up the possibility of experiencing a sexual complementarity—with the accompanying risk of the inevitable narcissistic wound of rejection.

To make such an approach takes a certain security, and the importance of the adolescent's peer group is that it is partly this that provides the essential security. To encounter the inexpressibly different other, adolescents seem to need a base in unquestioned similarity in order to have someone with whom they can lick their wounds. They will also carry with them what they have seen and experienced of their parents' relationship and its sexual characteristics. There is a very real sense that the acorn never falls far from the tree.

But it never coincides with the tree—a difference has to be accepted by the parents, which is not always easy. Many parents report that their mid-adolescents are like strangers to them because they seem so different from their former childhood selves. With the passing of mid-adolescence, these "strangers" to their parents increasingly become others in their own right. As this process gathers pace, parents can have one of the abiding satisfactions of having children: experiencing these "strangers" becoming very significant others in their lives as they grow older.

10

a time of tumult, torment, and promise

In this final chapter, I wish to draw together a number of strands and observe some common themes in the mid-adolescent's relationship with family, peers, and the "stranger" implied by beginning to enter the adult world. D. H. Lawrence called adolescence the "hour of the stranger", and with this he captured something important both about mid-adolescents' changing experience of themselves and others as they grow towards maturity and something of parents' experience of their child as puberty turns their once familiar offspring into someone new and unfamiliar. When he says "let the stranger enter the soul", we must accept that there is no need for permission being granted here. With the arrival of puberty, the "stranger" structures the adolescent's mind in a way that is irreversible. Thus, the adolescent becomes initially a stranger to himself, parents discover that there is a stranger in their midst, and the adolescent suddenly has the potential to discover a stranger who will become a significant other in their life.

There is no adolescent without parents

Just as there is no baby without a mother, so there is no adolescent without parents, whether they be in daily contact with their child or have been separated from them since birth. The effect is that mid-adolescents situate themselves in the generations because of the irreversible changes that take place in their sense of themselves with the arrival of puberty. Being biologically able to reproduce creates a new sense of self, with a potentially eager anticipation of the future and a dread of new responsibilities and demands. It also creates a tremendous shift in the way the parents' relationship is seen by their children.

While sociological research suggests that the majority of mid-adolescents negotiate the process of reaching towards maturity without externally exhibiting any sign that they are being disturbed by the process, the fact is that with the arrival of puberty a qualitative change occurs in their bodies. There is also a change in how developing adolescents think and feel; how they relate to others and the ways in which they experience things that worry them; how they view the past and the future, and how they react to the passing of childhood. As the education system prepares them for the demands of adult life, the implied challenge to the patterns of behaviour developed as they grew through their pre-pubertal years can create reactions ranging from resistance and efforts to escape to a pronounced flowering of abilities and potential. What is difficult to predict is how each individual adolescent will develop in the individual case.

Parents, too, will find that as their mid-adolescent grows towards maturity, they will encounter a stranger with whom they may sometimes be in sympathy, but whom at other times they may deeply resent and at times even loathe. Tumult may therefore not be confined to the adolescent's internal experience but also between parents and their adolescent children. As their children develop into adults and engage more fully with the outside world, parents encounter new situations. The issue often concerns finding the appropriate balance between protection from and exposure to the realities of the world.

The developing nature of the mid-adolescent, and the difficulty parents have in establishing what is appropriate objectively, means that much parental judgement will have to be based on intuition. This inevitably means that any parent will—*and can do no other than*—fall back on their own experience of adolescence, which will differ from that of their children. How parents imagine what is right for their children must be based on their knowledge of their child, their awareness of the world in which they all live, and their aspirations for their child.

But what is also involved is the degree to which they are prepared to take responsibility for the parenting of their children. The question of how society is going to support parents in this endeavour is then posed, which means that all legislation governing parental responsibility has to find a balance between support and sanction. In this respect, society is no different from parents, who also have to find a balance with which they are happy and which they can successfully exercise. This will run up against and sometimes conflict profoundly with the attitude of their children, who are developing a mind of their own as they reach towards their own sense of maturity.

Encountering the stranger

The fundamental idea in this book derives from Lawrence's idea of the "hour of the stranger". This stranger is encountered both by adolescents and by their families, as they will all will feel different and will, therefore, at times be in some sense strangers both to themselves and to their families and others immediately around them.

The second idea is that adolescents are on a trajectory from which they cannot escape, brought about by society in interaction with their individual psychic and biological processes. Adolescents will assign meaning to their experience of this process of trajectory, and they will communicate this meaning to the world around them.

Third, cognitive changes create a new potential for both encountering and understanding these strangers as individuals in their own right. The point of the prisoner's dilemma is to demonstrate that in order for an individual to know themselves, they must take into account not only what others seem to be like but also what they do in relation to them and *what they do not do.* Once the possibility has been grasped that the inertia of others means that they do not know who they are, then a window is opened into the psychic life of others. This learning takes time, and the time it takes is unavoidable. The time it will take for any one individual cannot be predicted.

This pattern of psychological development will be seen in the sexual behaviour of the mid-adolescent, the so-called psychosocial disturbances of adolescence, the kinds of disturbed emotions and behaviour that adolescents display in the process of growing to maturity. It can also be demonstrated in the kinds of cruelties that adolescents show towards one another, as discussed in chapter 8.

Narrowing our focus down onto mid-adolescence and defining this, for convenience's sake, as the years between 14 and 17, we may say that following the onset of puberty the process of growing away from the parents is shown by the growing importance of the peer group and the progressive testing of rules and boundaries.

Early adolescence can be thought of as a time when the consequences of the arrival of the sexual body are to be absorbed and a start made on the incorporation of this fact, in all its ramifications, into the adolescent's sense of themselves. Mid-adolescence brings *the stranger* into this process of absorption, because one of the consequences of puberty is that the opposite sex acquires a whole new significance, just as does the adolescent's body. The anxieties created by this psychological fact mean that others are necessary to help bear these anxiee home provided by parents and family no longer quite the same way. This is not to say that the parents and family become irrelevant, even if parents and family may sometimes feel irrelevant to their adolescent children. To the adolescent, parents and family may provide a haven, but they are not where the action is. Small wonder the home seems to be treated like a hotel: it is the base from which to encounter the world. If this base is threatened, then the adolescent will search for another or else stay inside the home to keep watch for any threats to their security.

Silence and the stranger

The dilemma for the mid-adolescent, then, is to be able to test and experiment as they grow towards maturity and not only see the effects of their actions on others but feel the anxieties that others experience as they take these actions. The boy asking a girl out on a first date risks rebuff and a blow to his dignity if refused. In the moment he has no way of knowing for certain what the reply will be and, if rebuffed, not much to fall back on in understanding the reason for the rebuff other than his own insecurities about himself and all the means he has to cope with these insecurities. Girls will be in the same position, even if waiting to be asked—if that is the local norm. Each may envy and resent the other for the imagined "power" of their position. Some find this overwhelming and take a long time to dare to take the risk.

One's mates are crucial in negotiating this narcissistic crisis. Parents may or may not be aware of these struggles in their adolescent children. Even if they are, they may not be seen by their children as being able to "understand", perhaps because they will be seen as never having had to experience such uncertainty (because they are unconsciously imagined to have always been an "item"). Few things can be more difficult for an adult than trying to convince an anxious mid-adolescent that those of the opposite sex are as anxious as he or she is. Unconsciously the message is always: "What do you know . . . you old crusty?" There is no dodging the anxiety stirred by the encounter with the "stranger", and nothing more patronizing than to dismiss it.

Another possibility can be that an adolescent wants to keep this part of their life a secret from their parents, because it is believed they will disapprove. We saw earlier that the breaking of the infantile ties of childhood to the parents entails that parents must be thought of as disapproving as these ties are broken. The resistance to breaking away that the adolescent sees—or in some cases creates—in his parents can be very largely based on the adolescent's own anxieties. This can be too difficult to acknowledge, particularly if the temptation to give in to these anxieties is strong. We then have the adolescent who can't leave home.

As a result, adolescents wrestling with these anxieties often feel that they should be able to deal with them on their own. This is because they believe that everyone else their age does so, and they themselves would be wimps if they needed help. All these anxieties make the process of sex education fraught with difficulty because of the anxieties that are evoked in both parents and their adolescent children at the prospect of their being or becoming sexually active. And yet it is this very absence of adequate sex education that contributes to it being the social problem that it has become in some societies.

In this society, perhaps, nowhere is the absence of proper adult authority more visible than in matters of sex education. The problems for all concerned are clearly demonstrated by the development of the idea of "Gillick competence". All the known facts on adolescent sexual behaviour suggest that many adolescents use their bodies to express their antisocial tendency much as do those who commit acts of criminal behaviour, and possibly for very similar reasons. We also note that the age–crime curve that seems a universal phenomenon regardless of culture indicates that all adolescents react in some way to the end of childhood and the loss of the old infantile ties to the parents. If this loss can feel somehow as if childhood has been stolen from adolescents by the adult world, then perhaps we should not be surprised at the existence of the age–crime phenomenon.

Such thoughts might be rather sobering for the parental generation used to media that bemoan the "wronging of the ancientry" by modern youth. Yet it seems possible that the "stranger" whom parents encounter in their adolescent children is the counterpart of the stranger whom adolescents encounter as they pass through mid-adolescence. This stranger can be just as frightening as the one encountered by their children, but also just as fascinating and full of promise.

The point of articulating these matters in terms of "the stranger" is that it may provide some means for the generations to communicate with each other in terms that they both understand at times when it can seem that there is a huge gulf between them. Even if both parents and adolescents can feel that each is a stranger to the other, it seems both sides are more willing to seek to be understood than it might often appear. Adolescents and their parents are all facing something new in the demands on them for change and development. We have readily observed the paradoxical experience of the mid-adolescent eagerly looking to the future while reluctantly leaving childhood. We have seen how this paradox is expressed through antisocial behaviour and the emergence of various kinds of mental disturbance. We have seen how it has been presented dramatically in *Romeo and Juliet* and in literature in *Le Blé en Herbe.* We seem to have come to the conclusion that the issue, both for adolescents and for their parents, is whether this stranger—implied by the imperative of the adolescent accepting change and development—is to be welcomed or, as far as is possible, avoided.

References

Bazalgette, J. (1978). *School Life and Work Life: A Study of Transition in the Inner City.* London: Hutchinson.

Brien, J., & Fairbairn, I. (1996). *Pregnancy and Abortion Counselling.* London: Routledge.

Colette, S.-G. (1969). *Le Blé en Herbe.* Paris: Flammarion. [English translation: *Green Wheat.* Louisville, KY: Sarabande Books, 2004.]

Coleman, J., & Schofield, J. (2003). *Key Data on Adolescence 2003.* Brighton: Trust for the Study of Adolescence.

Dalsimer, K. (1986). *Female Adolescence: Psychoanalytic Reflections on Literature.* New Haven, CT/London: Yale University Press.

Erikson, E. (1950). *Childhood and Society.* Harmondsworth: Penguin.

Farrington, D. P., Gallagher, B., Morley, L., St. Ledger, R. J., & & West, D. J. (1986). Unemployment, school leaving and crime. *British Journal of Criminology, 26*: 335–356.

Farrington, D. P. (1995). The challenge of teenage antisocial behaviour. In: M. Rutter (Ed.), *Psychosocial Disturbances in Young People.* Cambridge: Cambridge University Press.

Freud, A. (1949) On certain difficulties in the preadolescent's relation to his parents. *Writings, Vol. 4* (pp. 95–106). New York: International Universities Press, 1968.

Fussell, P. (2004). *The Boys' Crusade.* London: Weidenfeld & Nicholson.

Gottfredson, M. R., & Hirshi, T. (1990). *A General Theory of Crime.* Stanford, CA: Stanford University Press.

Guillebaud, J. (1993). *Conception: Your Questions Answered.* London: Churchill Livingstone.

Hawton, K., Fagg J., Simkin, S., Bate, E., & Bond, A. (2000). Deliberate self-harm in adolescents in Oxford 1985–95. *Journal of Adolescence, 23*: 47–55.

Larson, R. (2002) *Adolescent's Preparation for the Future: Perils and Promise.* Ann Arbor, MI: The Society for Research on Adolescence.

Lawrence, D. H. (1923). *Fantasia of the Unconscious.* London: Heinemann.

Magnusson, D., & Bergman, L. R. (1988). A pattern approach to the study of pathways from childhood to adulthood. In: L. N. Robins & M. Rutter (Eds.), *Straight and Devious Pathways from Childhood to Adulthood.* Cambridge: Cambridge University Press.

Mead, M. (1930). *Growing Up in New Guinea.* New York: HarperCollins.

Millstein, S. G., Petersen, A. C., & Nightingale, E. O. (Eds.) (1996). *Promoting the Health of Adolescents.* New York: Oxford University Press.

O'Moore, A., & Hillery, B. (1989). Bullying in Dublin schools. *Irish Journal of Psychology, 10*: 426–441.

Piaget, J. (1950). *The Psychology of Intelligence.* London: Routledge & Kegan Paul.

Rainer, E., Joyce, A., Rose, J. S., Twyman, M., & Clulow, C. (2005). *Human Development* (4th edition). London: Routledge.

Rutter, M., & Giller, H. (1983). *Juvenile Delinquency: Patterns and Trends.* Harmondsworth: Penguin.

Salinger, J. D. (1951). *The Catcher in the Rye.* London: Hamish Hamilton.

Santrock, J. (1999). *Life-Span Development.* New York: McGraw-Hill College.

Smith, P. K., & Myron-Wilson, R. (1998). Parenting and school bullying. *Clinical Child Psychology and Psychiatry. 3*: 405–417.

Van Heeswyck, P. (1997). *Analysing Adolescence.* London: Sheldon Press

Wellings, K., Nanchahal, K., Macdowall, W., McManus, S., Erens, R., Mercer, C. H., Johnson, A. M., Copas, A. J., Korovessis, C., Fenton, K. A., & Field, J. (2001). Sexual behaviour in Britain: Early heterosexual experience. *The Lancet, 358*: 1843–1850.

Winnicott, D. W. (1956). The antisocial tendency. In: *Through Paediatrics to Psychoanalysis.* London: Hogarth, 1958.

Winnicott, D. W. (1968). Contemporary concepts of adolescent development and their implications for higher education. In: *Playing and Reality.* London: Tavistock, 1971.

Index